SICK
SUCCESS

SICK

THE ENTREPRENEUR'S
PRESCRIPTIONS FOR TURNING
PAIN INTO PURPOSE & PROFIT

SUCCESS

HILARY JASTRAM

SOUND WISDOM
P.O. Box 310
Shippensburg, PA 17257-0310

For more information on publishing and distribution rights, call 717-530-2122 or info@soundwisdom.com.

Quantity Sales. Special discounts are available on quantity purchases by corporations, associations, and others. For details, contact the Sales Department at Sound Wisdom.

While efforts have been made to verify information contained in this publication, neither the author nor the publisher assumes any responsibility for errors, inaccuracies, or omissions.

While this publication is chock-full of useful, practical information, it is not intended to be legal or accounting advice. All readers are advised to seek competent lawyers and accountants to follow laws and regulations that may apply to specific situations.

The reader of this publication assumes responsibility for the use of the information. The author and publisher assume no responsibility or liability whatsoever on the behalf of the reader of this publication.

ISBN 13 TP: 978-1-64095-030-6
ISBN 13 Ebook: 978-1-64095-031-3

For Worldwide Distribution, Printed in the U.S.A.
1 2 3 4 5 6 7 8 / 21 20 19 18

Cover and bio photo by Jen Kelly/KeliComm Headshots
Interior design by Susan Ramundo

DEDICATION

To all the people who have been suddenly thrown off their path by illness or accident. Accept the invitation into your new reality, knowing it may lead to the fulfillment of your deepest dreams.

CONTENTS

FOREWORD

Once upon a time, I wrote blog posts and books and threw them up on my site or rushed to publish them. It was a matter of "good enough" as I rushed through my work. Then one day, I met Hilary. I don't remember exactly how we met or who it was that introduced us, but shortly after, Hilary came to me and said, "I'd like to reedit your books for you." At first, I thought she was just being nice and trying to weasel her way into my life, to get me to turn over my prospects or send her referrals. I was naturally skeptical. Now, that's exactly what's happened! I send Hilary every referral I get. She's actually done the editing of every single blog post that I've ever written. Every article in *Forbes*, every article in *Huffington Post*, every post on Hardcore Closer, every book uploaded to Amazon, Hilary is my wordsmith.

I know Hilary as Hil-Dawg. That's the nickname I've given her, and it's what we call her over here at Break Free Academy. Hil-Dawg has been a blessing to me, and this book's going to be a blessing to you 'cause she's got a hell of a story to tell.

Since the first time we connected, I've watched Hilary grow. Over two years ago, she was a delicate snowflake looking to blame everybody else for her problems. She would accuse people of this and that and was offended by so many things. One day, she and I had a come-to-Jesus meeting where I said, "Hilary, you're a badass. It's time for you to start acting like it."

At first, I think she told me to pound sand 10 ways from Sunday, but then the truth sunk in, and she came back to me and said, "You know what? You're right. I've gotta harden up." That was the point when she began making different decisions about her life and business. I was there to witness the changes she made, and I have watched her business grow exponentially as a result. I have also watched her attitude improve exponentially. I have watched her quality of life elevate to a level she never thought she could see. She's married to the man of her dreams. Her business is flourishing and busier than ever. She no longer spends her time looking for offenses, and now (my favorite change), she's even written a book. This time it's nonfiction and it's her story. Her story is inspiring because Hilary's an inspiring person. She's a detail-oriented person, too, so you know the book's going to be grammatically correct and properly spelled. That's what she does.

I can't say enough about my friend, Hil-Dawg. She's seen me go through some rough times with a bad attitude. She's seen my good attitude carry me through good times as well, and she's always been there for me.

In this book, you'll learn the details of her life and her experiences. You'll learn what she's had to overcome in her lifetime. The reason she wrote this book is for you to learn from those experiences. So, you will gain wisdom and then go out there and avoid making the same mistakes. Instead, you will prosper.

I know Hilary's heart, and that's all she wants for anybody: for everybody to enjoy success. That's why she's so enthusiastic about helping people get their books published and sold because she wants people to be successful. It's why she started her nonprofit, Sick Biz: to help chronically ill and disabled entrepreneurs. She truly cares, and I truly care about my friend, Hilary. I couldn't be prouder of her for writing this book, and I'm honored that she asked me to write the foreword for it.

Savor this book. We are both extremely glad you've gotten your hands on it. You're in for a treat because these chapters have all the details of her journey and contain many different ways you can apply the content to improve your own life.

Ryan Stewman
CEO, Hardcore Closer

INTRODUCTION

Dear warts and all...

You're probably wondering why I started the introduction this way... But it makes sense when you realize this book is about learning to love yourself throughout your life and healing to the point where you can operate and flourish in your own business.

Our timeline on this Earth is littered with the challenge to love ourselves. We carry our doubts into every facet of our lives, and this is especially true if we have had no or few good models from our childhood. I don't include the painful and, sometimes, agonizing parts of my life to belabor them, create attention, or extend the misery. I am not including them to feel what I now know was misplaced negative drama for love. I refuse to do that anymore. That is not the type of attention I want. I don't think it is the type of attention anyone wants.

What I am about to share with you is based on relevance only. It is rooted in my survivor's spirit and the fact that I believe...scratch that...I KNOW what we go through is meant to feed and enlighten each other. When we unbolt ourselves from the expectations of what our lives are supposed to be and remain open to the changes that come barging in with no notice, we can walk toward intense empowerment. We can discover pain through purpose.

Let's go for a walk.

Section One

0–30ish: MY FORMATIVE YEARS

Chapter 1

MEMORIES CATCHING LIGHT

Many times, I have begun to write what people may consider my memoir only to revisit the draft and decide it was crap. I get hung up on telling my story. Self-doubts run rampant through my mind, determined to stop any sort of self-healing process. I might write about being a little girl at the age of four, and when I discovered my life wasn't all puppies and unicorns, then I figured nobody would care, and so I would delete it. I'd try again, and the cycle would continue until I stopped writing my story at all.

Now, I'm going to keep going even when I encounter the saggy-bottom middle. Even when my demons are tugging at my shirtsleeve and demanding that I dance with them. I will do my best to step out of the forest where I can't see the truth for the trees. Because we all have a story to tell.

This is mine.

• • •

It's 2018, and for the last year, I have seriously considered sending Stephen King a petition to adopt me. I was born in Kittery, Maine, so I feel an affinity and closeness to him since he lives in Maine. Mr. King entered my life when I was on a yearly family vacation at our cabin on the lake. A staple getaway, if you are a Minnesotan. My grandfather was reading the book *It*, and I would check the thinning width of the number of pages he had yet to read. I was anxious to get my hands on it, and my family always encouraged reading, so I knew that even though I was barely a teen, I would be allowed passage into the world of what would become my favorite author. His words were delicious. I lapped them up like they were strawberry cream pops. The worlds he created instilled in me that horror can live right in your very own life. Maybe that is why I became so attached? Years later, I would attend a live round table with him and Audrey Niffenegger, the author of the *Time Traveler's Wife*. While he was speaking and even though I was enamored, I left the auditorium, teetering in high-heeled boots up the stairs that led to the lobby. My phone was ringing. My boyfriend (now my husband) was deploying to Iraq that very day, and it was also his birthday. Only he could pull me away from Stephen King, who I've found endlessly fascinating. But I don't just admire his writing. I've also read he is a wonderful father. He has three children who are free, creative people, and his daughter is wheelchair bound. I am sure his heart broke over that development, but it also teaches me of his compassion. I relate again, as I sometimes use a chair, appropriately named, *The Silver Bullet*. An homage to Mr. King.

I had an outstanding father for a few years, and then something happened inside his brain as a result of choices he made and the limited tools he had access to, which did not allow him to understand boundaries and responsibility. When I was 13, he packed up his car and moved to the other side of the country. I didn't know enough to understand it would ever enter his mind to desert his children.

My mind flitters across many different topics when I remember growing up. I bounce from one memory to the next, much like the coveted monarch butterflies I used to capture religiously and put into recycled mayonnaise jars. If I close my eyes, I can still hear the sound screwing the lid on tight made, feel the grip of my hand around the scissors as I punched air holes in the top.

My story isn't a movie reel feeding out one event after the other in chronological disorder. I meant to write chronological order. But I'm leaving in my typo of "chronological disorder" because it's the purest truth I can impart.

From the ages of 0–11, life was "normal." Our family had not yet fallen prey to the increasing statistic of marriages ending in divorce. We were a unit, and to my immature brain, it seemed we would last forever.

Chapter 2

FORMATIVE TO FORMLESS

Of the 14 various states of houses and rooms I would occupy before I was 20, New Hampshire provided my first homes, Pease Air Force Base and then our house in Dover.

I was born at a military hospital in Kittery, Maine, although we lived on an Air Force base in New Hampshire. It is how I began life, crossing over a bridge, and that notion of spanning one stage to the next continues to follow me through life. I always seem to be in some sort of flux or crossing over into what's waiting next. It has taken a very long time to even welcome the alien feeling of staying put, whether that describes moving into new homes, rotating significant others, jobs, or family members coming in and out, my life has been one bridge after another.

We lived on the base for a few years and then moved to the Dover fourplex. Our house was Victorian inspired, butter yellow with white trim. My sister and I shared a room. She was my best friend, and I wanted our relationship to continue forever.

We plucked the wiggling, fat monarch caterpillars off the neighbor's chain link fence, then grabbed a fistful of milkweed stems that snapped open and spilled sticky juice on our hands. Condiment jars, sticks, and clumps of grass worked beautifully to house our beasties. We would sit on the warm floor of the sunroom as the rays kissed our shoulders, studying the process of the caterpillar becoming a butterfly. It was a messy and unglamorous change but fascinating because when the caterpillar was engulfed in the cocoon, we knew surreal change was imminent. Once we put a caterpillar into a ketchup bottle, and when it emerged, it had to squeeze through the skinny neck to dry its wings. It crushed a wing as it escaped and became a butterfly that could only eternally hop and never fly. I still think of the message that little bug carries and remember being sad we had caused the injury from which it would never recover. Is there anything so tragic as a butterfly who can't fly?

I was a weird little kid who also collected frogs that I kept in pickle jars shoved under the porch and hidden in the cool dirt. With rocks digging into my knees, I would reach through the lattice and touch the cold glass and watch my frog prisoners. It didn't occur to me I was depriving them of a life they might want to live in the nearby ponds and long grass. I thought I did an excellent job taking care of them in their glass frog zoo until one hopped out of my reach and wound up plastered on a neighbor's driveway after she'd driven over it. I peeled the body up and took it into the house, weeping about my lost friend, his green form petrified and mashed into a thin, flat disk. When I showed my parents my dead friend, my dad laughed. He had a deep and contagious roar. It boomed from the pit of his belly, and I loved hearing it because it was reassuring to me. That sound was the only one I wanted to hear, and I didn't hear it enough.

As I held my frog out and sensed the wet tear tracks on my face, I wondered, *Why is he laughing at me?* But as I would learn to do, I quickly sucked up the rest of my tears and joined in the joke, even though my young heart ached.

As easily as he would laugh, I quickly learned not to tangle with his temper.

One night at dinner, his face, inches away from mine, resembled a beefsteak tomato. His olive complexion boiled into red. The rush of warm spittle mist from his screaming caused me to howl louder as he demanded I eat my dinner. I shoveled in a cold glump of weenies and beans. The combination of the juices from the beans and hotdogs was unpalatable, and I gagged as I held the food in my mouth and wished I could swallow. But I couldn't. Instead, I gagged repeatedly, struggling to catch my breath, while he still hollered and threatened to spank me. I don't know how the night ended. I may have blocked it out, but in my four-year-old estimation, I was suffocating while one of the people I loved most in the world demonstrated outright hate and revulsion. I was careful eating after that as I waited for a repeat session and did everything I could think of to never get him mad. I don't know where my mom was. I don't know if she was even aware of what had happened. And I surmise this was the beginning of my vomiting phobia.

You don't understand the intricacies of living with a person so prone to rage, how you can have one minute of peace and whooshing joy and another of terror, unless you have lived with an abuser. We did have amazing moments. Once I told my dad I wanted to go up in a helicopter, and he chartered one. Then just he and I hit the air. I was dazzled as I leaned forward and drank up all the scenery outside the curved windows. My heart was in danger of bursting because I felt so special, and as a small kid, I was in love with my father. He was handsome and perfect with near black hair and emerald eyes. He told us about nature and took us blueberry picking where we discussed the danger of being eaten by bears. He brought us skiing and fishing, and we watched him tie flies with doll-sized scissors. My young life was an odd paradox of panic and emotional paralysis when he was in a lather and a craving for his love that was so strong it physically hurt when he wasn't.

When I was six years old, the Air Force moved us to Norfolk, Virginia. This is why I don't sound like a genuine Minnesotan but a mash-up of Eastern and Midwestern.

The years between one and seven were unremarkable and stable. My dedicated stay-at-home mother remembered birthdays and honored my sister and me with homemade cakes. One year, my orange cake had a jack-o'-lantern face. The snapshot of my wide grin as I posed with the cake reminds me of simple bliss.

Mom had to walk us to school, which loomed up as we crossed the busy, double-lane street. I recall my kindergarten teacher's soft voice with the slight authoritative edge. I was the only person in the advanced reading class, and the primer taught me "cat" and "bat." My days were full of coloring, drawing, playing with my golden, overstuffed dog Rover, and dodging cockroaches in our kitchen. I passed elaborate webs owned by yellow and black garden spiders in the front yard and was never afraid but fascinated. We endured a flood that sent my sister leaping out of bed and into my parents' room hollering 'The water's up to the windows!" as she ran. Life was pleasing as I traipsed along behind my mom wherever she went, dragging my rubber alligator tied to a shoelace.

When we moved to Minnesota, mom was elated because she had her family back. We had visited there once when my uncle was sick, my sister and I playing foosball in the rec area of the hospital. The adults could visit him, but we were not allowed in his room. The tang of ammonia on the stark floors prickled our noses. Then I learned he had died. I talk to him sometimes and wonder if he remembers me...

We traveled in an extended-length station wagon named Old Blue when we made the journey to St. Paul. Blue's jump seats faced the back window, and my sister and I watched the world pull away as we moved from state to state.

We lived in an apartment on Scudder Street in St. Paul, and my sister and I divided up our room with tape that we stuck down on the middle of the floor. If you were on the side without the door, you had to jump over the tape and land on the carpet in the area where the door was. We became guinea-pig crazy around that time when I was allowed to keep the class pet, Brownshoe, permanently. His orange and white fur stuck up in tufts all over his body, and I am sure as a gregarious child, I scared him to death. For years, we were never without our guinea pigs. They smelled like freshly ripped newspaper and wheat pellets—the scent of vitamins. I loved holding their chunky bodies that were soft and warm and poking at their tiny pink feet. Our apartment was surrounded by older homes that we would imagine were haunted. In fall, we would kick the leaves on the sidewalk as we made our way to the park, and I still love that smell of wet and dry and how it reminds me of the intoxicating meaning of life. My mother worked at a medical clinic by now, and she would remain there for the next 30+ years. I missed her when she was gone and felt I had taken advantage of her presence. Almost every day, I would call her to ask if I could have an orange or toast after school. If she was busy at work, one of the other moms would give me permission to eat, and we would laugh about that when she got home.

My mother was a gorgeous blonde with the softest, most flower-fragrant hair who smiled and laughed a lot. She was easily the most stunning mother out of any of my classmates'. We were her center. I could tell it by the way she brushed my hair and made sure our homework was done and handed in. I was a voracious reader, and mom always took us to the library. There we would pick out books I would dive into. I read *Benji*, Laura Ingalls Wilder, Nancy Drew, *Mrs. Piggle-Wiggle*, and all the Judy Blume books I could devour. I had just learned how to do a standing flip and land on my heels in my gymnastics class when my parents informed us we were moving because they had bought a house.

Our house on Minnehaha had four bedrooms upstairs and another bedroom on the main floor that was mine for a while after the ceiling in my original bedroom caved in during a slumber party. The cracked and damp plaster crumbled all over the sleeping bag of the girl I had been trying to impress. My first-floor bedroom overlooked a garden nook with snapdragons that persevered despite knee-high weeds. If I slid back the paneling of one wall in my room, I would see the stair spindles. We only lived in this house for about a year, but it represents the pivotal end of everything that had made me feel secure.

The housing market's astronomical 20%-plus rates and virulent unemployment caused us to lose our dream house. When my dad was laid off, he saw other possibilities for making money. But this new reality came only after he had applied to heaps of opportunities and been turned down. No longer would he take us to his work and show my sister and me the computer that swallowed up a whole room. Now, he stayed at home and drew still life art, sold rare coins, and told his girls he was going to build a mini-replica dollhouse that would be identical to our home. I was quite excited when he made this announcement and barely resisted hopping up and down as I had never had a dollhouse. Our life changed, gradually and then all at once, until everything we knew and could count on was gone. As I reflect now, I know what we went through was about survival, not about deliberate pain and hurt. But it hurt anyway. We were losing the house we had put our hopes into, going from remodeling and scraping the paint off wood slats using a small propane torch to packing boxes. I was entranced by the cloying scent of the paint bubbling up and the way it peeled off so cleanly. We perched on ladders outside the bay windows of the dining room, inhaling the fumes and having a great ol' time. The summer before, we had trained a squirrel with a fab white mohawk named Spot to come and take nuts out of our hands as we sat on the back stoop. Then Spot tried to get in the house, and my sister and I squealed and slipped through the door just in time to look out and see him hanging on the screen door that flapped in the wind. I was afraid Spot would bite us. But he only licked my toe. Spot was found dead shortly after, flattened on the sidewalk. We would also have to leave behind our cat Mallory that had brain damage and left streaks of orange feces on the carpet. My dad regularly bowled her into the radiator, and I can still hear the sound her body made as it struck metal. I was horrified and said nothing as I watched her shake off her pain and walk away, my face tight and hot from holding back tears. I don't remember what happened to her. But I loved her, and one day she was gone. Shortly after, I sneaked a bewitching calico I called Muff in the door. She curled up once or twice on my bed before we moved and left her at the empty house. Then she got pregnant. One day, I walked from our new duplex to the old house looking for her. I called her name, clucked my tongue, and she appeared through wisps of grass, running toward me, dragging her baby behind her, still attached by the cord. The kitten was dead, and Muff had no idea. As I scrambled away from her, I fell down our little hill in the front yard, slicing my leg open on a rock. I never saw her again. My little sister was also born during that year, and when she was less than a year old, I was kept home from school to watch her one day. Her crying frustrated me so badly I flung her walker across our hardwood floor. She only flew about 10 feet, but I was horrified at the temper bubbling up inside me. I loved her, and I wanted to take care of her. When she was sick one night and my parents left to take her to the hospital, I stayed behind and sung church hymns in my clearest, sweetest voice. Despite the moments when I felt such undeniable compassion, I wondered if I would become like my father. I wondered if I would hate myself.

The panic attacks that continue to ravage my existence, although far less frequently now, developed. I was fearful of vomiting and would panic if I even suspected I was sick. My dad would always take care of me, dumping out my puke bowl and staying up with me at night. He picked me up once at a Girl Scout sleepover when I felt the hot wave of anxiety roll through me. The troop leader grabbed a casserole dish, and I thought, *What a ridiculous thing to barf in.* In this one jam-packed year, when life's lessons flew in my face too often, we also transferred schools. On one of the first days I was there, I learned about a girl who had gone missing and whose body had been found in a dumpster. My friends had been friends with her. Then her family moved away, but they continued to try and work out the details of what happened. I'm sure they were attempting to create distance between themselves and her death to feel safer. I did that, too. I told myself that she had been taken in different part of town where I didn't go, and I made a promise inside that I would never leave during a church service or go anywhere without my parents. In some way, I figured that tragedy is like a lightning strike. It doesn't hit in the same place. Horror had passed through our little nook of the world, and it hadn't taken me, so we could get back to normal. I was relieved when the topic in the schoolyard changed from hearing details about her abduction that froze me solid, to who was going to attempt the double-dutch record that day.

In this home, we went from rich spaghetti sauce and meatballs cooking on the stove all day to hunting in the cupboard for what had been brought home from the food donation place. On good days, my parents would take out cans of SpaghettiOs from the mismatched grocery bags that had been given from the various, local grocery stores in the area. We went from heating every part of our residence to huddling in the kitchen with the oven door open and the two adjoining doors shut to trap in the heat. The oil used to heat the home in the late '80s cost a couple thousand dollars a month. My parents set themselves up for failure with that house. It was exciting to live in it and show my friends my impressive home, but it was not a sustainable decision and was the first tipping point.

In the duplex, located five blocks away from our former dream house, life got worse. Our electricity was shut off, and we had to take baths in the dark. We fried the fridge's motor from running it on an extension cord and were forced to store our milk and bologna in the snow on our one-chair balcony. I was painfully embarrassed by this stage in my life. We had no phone, and I couldn't talk to friends, and I never let anyone come over because I was petrified they would learn about the conditions we lived in. On my birthday, I was told no one could afford anything for me, and instead a neighbor made me a cake. I went to bed crying and stared out the window of the attic dormer from my bed. I was so close that I could touch my nose to the dusty screen and turn my head to gaze into the indigo sky. As I laid there, the crisp autumn breeze washing over my tearstained face, I got lost in a million stars and forgot I was forgotten.

Once my dad didn't come home for three days, and when I was taking one of my dark baths, I heard my mother crying in the other room. She asked him where he had been, and from the theme of the conversation, I could tell he was wheedling his way through an answer although I hadn't yet had full exposure to the level of poisonous manipulation he would later achieve. But I could sense a new personality peeking around the edges of my father's psyche. We didn't stay long in the duplex before next moving into a little stucco house, and we did it in the middle of the night.

I was 13 years old, retching from exhaustion, when we hustled under the cover of darkness to a new house, I'm assuming, to avoid our old landlord. As I wiped the wetness from under my eyes and crouched over the bowl, dad had a rare moment of compassion and sent me to bed. I was thankful, as I shambled away, that he did not respond in anger. Once, and I don't remember the context of our conversation, he remarked with a slight grin, "When I get angry, I see people as objects that must be destroyed."

Living with an angry and controlling father impacted my life in ways I wasn't aware of at the time. It conditioned me to use a quiet voice when I was in public or with people I didn't know and to phrase myself in ways that would prevent conflict. I censored my true feelings and learned to become a peacekeeper so I could control the volatility of situations.

A few months after moving in, my dad called me over to his old, disgusting plaid recliner. I didn't like to get too close as he always wore perspiration-stained wife beaters and never stopped smoking. He asked me how I would feel if he left and if I thought he should divorce my mom. I remember thinking, *We have made it as a family. We're the only family out of my friends who aren't divorced. My response will determine the future of us.* Always trying to live ripple-free, I told him lots of families do it and I wanted him to feel better. But I knew whatever the decision, it would be my fault. And I felt compelled to help him out of his torturous mind as I perched on the edge of the chair arm and searched my limited and addled brain for the right answer. I wanted him to still love me despite what I had to say, but I also wanted to give him the right answer that would make him feel better, even though I was only thirteen.

As I looked into his hazel eyes with the faint etchings of crinkles at the edges, I noticed a softening. *He didn't know the answer he wanted me to tell him.* It was a very short conversation. I hopped off the arm of the chair after blurting out my thoughts and with a sharp lump in my throat, my heart thumping in my ears, held my tears until I was safely in my room.

I don't believe my dad knew what he was asking of his child because I don't believe he was prepared for his own parenthood. My childhood is spotted with moments that, when I extrapolate forward, I couldn't imagine my children bearing.

Right before he pulled away from our house, he told my sister and me he would always be a bicycle ride away. California is not a bicycle ride away from Minnesota. Over the years, he would forget our birthdays and what grades we were in. He would lie more than he would tell the truth, and the fallout from his decision, I believe, would cause the gradual demise of his sanity. He was diagnosed with manic depressive disorder and spent time in prison for being a perv. We don't talk now, but even though our relationship was pure hell at points, I have to remember this is not the full measure of a person, no matter the depth of their sickness. We had good times, some of which I've named here.

I didn't see mom a lot, and I entered a phase where I probably didn't want to. Anger was nibbling at me. I had been favored and loved and had experienced some very cool things like living near the ocean, skiing, and camping, but now life had been stripped of those niceties, and it would never be the same.

We left our little house and moved into another duplex. I shared a room with my sister before she left to live with my father. My mother met a man and spent many nights away, and I turned to drinking and partying. I wouldn't listen, and I did what I wanted. When I was 16, I tried to kill myself by taking eight Advil pills in a bathroom stall at school. I didn't understand it wouldn't kill me; in my mind, it was going to. I never told a soul. But instead, I took the pills and waited, having accepted my fate. I realize now this is a bittersweet story, and it's even comical. I joke that my body must've felt terrific that day. No aches or pains! But I remember the feeling of finality and the thought that no one would care if I simply disappeared. I was learning I was forgettable and that love had conditions.

I continued ditching, drinking, and partying, and because of the lack of parental presence, I reacted with rage whenever my mom questioned anything about my life. I was furious she wasn't there and thought she had zero right to tell me what to do. I disobeyed her to her face, and one day we got into a screaming and physical fight as she shampooed the rug in the living room. Weightless suds flew around us like huge snowflakes as I sought to be loved and to win love, to be right and validated. Instead, a deeper gulf cracked my foundation. Mom kept the electricity running and the phone on. She got dinners on the table and even let us have a cat, which then had three kittens, all of which had fleas. We gave them a bath in the sink, and the fleas crawled to the tops of their heads. After those kittens were given away, I turned my attention to a small white mouse named Rascal who lived on the back of the toilet in a cage. I went to work at a grocery store and walked about a mile there and back every day. I loved being a cashier and talking to all the customers. I especially adored helping one gentleman who couldn't talk, was in a wheelchair, and wore a pointer on his head to tap out the names of the items he needed. We would roll and shop. He smelled faintly of antiseptic, and I tried to make him smile every time he came in. By now, I had been flashed twice in my life, had been assaulted by a date, had lived on the ground floor apartment with two drug dealers, and was looking for love in all the dysfunctional places, even betraying some of my closest friends with their boyfriends to find anyone who gave a crap about me. I bought my own toiletries, tampons and the like, walked everywhere, and discovered creative writing and theater. On stage, although I was never picked for the major parts, I was reminded that people could see me. I was the feature editor for the newspaper and tried to break shocking stories. I missed 31 days of creative writing class and graduated anyway only because the teacher told me I had aptitude. Since we had moved from St. Paul to Minneapolis in my senior year to live in my great-grandma's old house, I was damned if I was going to attend another school. So, I established an account with a local cab company and paid them monthly to take me from my front doorstep to my old school. I did not drive and had no one to teach me. Although I did purchase a car that I had towed to our driveway, I would sit in it and listen to the radio as I smoked cigarettes. I would close my eyes and allow myself to be abducted into a different existence. I tried to belong but couldn't. At 20, I got pregnant, stayed a few nights in a wayward girls' home, and suffered being unable to take care of my child, who was loved by multiple people until I could get it together and finally grow up for him. We stayed in the house until my son was about one year old, and then I placed him with his father, so I could work two jobs and get back on my feet. I wanted to make a better life for us. He deserved it. I will never stop making it up to my son for those moments in my life where I was absolutely robbed of bonding time. I didn't know I had a right to have a voice. Understand, I take responsibility for all my decisions. But as a twenty-something, I had no idea I could even stand up for myself or that I could make decisions for my child and me. I just wanted life to continue and to be a good mother.

When my kid lived with his dad, I had a fling with the bosses and other employees at these places and burned bridges as soon as I crossed them.

I was homeless for two months and stayed with a revolving stable of people and boyfriends, never accepting the gravity of my situation and trundling around in my old Honda Accord. Then I moved in with my aunt and uncle and became part of their family. My bedroom was on the back end of the house with more windows than walls, and I loved every moment I spent there. I was secure, clean, loved, welcomed, and forever told my life and my son's were meaningful. When my little boy came to visit, we would play as I worried about nothing. Both my aunt and uncle were unflappable parents who were always smiling and laughing. They flirted as they passed each other in the kitchen and encouraged us all to eat at the table. I didn't have to hide snacks and could finally eat as much as I wanted until I was full.

My appetite as a kid had been ravenous, and I don't remember feeling full a lot. Once when I babysat for my aunt and uncle, I rustled around in the fridge until I found a Tupperware full of chopped-up cantaloupe. I took it with me into the living room where I was watching television since the kids had gone to bed. When the parents came home, they asked where the container was. I said, "I'm sorry. I ate it all. Couldn't help myself," then smiled sheepishly. My aunt replied incredulously, "That was an entire cantaloupe."

My time at my aunt and uncle's home was a respite from the ongoing change and trauma of what had become my existence and my son's as well. I had stopped running and could pause and reinvent survival. I had a break from adapting to life-altering changes I couldn't anticipate. These were the good times my spirit had craved.

I transitioned quickly into my first marriage and another child. I was a control freak trying to smile through gritted teeth and constantly doubted I could ever pull off marriage or motherhood. The echoes in my head of being told I was the cause of every bit of our family's pain, that left me gasping and sobbing over the toilet, wouldn't quiet.

My head asked me, *Just who do you think you are?* But I tried to ignore the voice. Now I know mothers do what they have to. Every moment of motherhood can feel like a crap-shoot, but as long as you don't go anywhere and you keep trying, you are doing alright. We stayed in the apartment for about a year, then bought our first house where I got pregnant with my daughter.

Our next home was located in the suburbs on a cul-de-sac and would take us through a divorce, another marriage and divorce, and then the moving in of my boyfriend, now my husband, Deacon. In this house, I caved into rageful moments, destroyed all the relationships I could, was fired from too many jobs because I felt I had been sent to be a crusader for coworkers. My eating disorder dove into a horrific state, and I raised my kids the best I could while writing my first novel. I had gone back to school and discovered for the first time, at the age of 32, that I was smart, even earning an A in physics. We eventually lost our home, which led us to a cozy farmhouse where we live now.

Chapter 3

THE FLIP SIDE OF SURVIVING

I had become easily able to pick up on when a situation with my father was escalating, and I had also discerned what I needed to do to de-escalate it. It seems people in those daily circumstances who live afraid have that ability.

Many memories of my childhood shouldn't be called memories. They might be labeled moments of endurance or training for life. I learned love can be conditional when you have a close family member with limited tools for coping. I learned to take my terror and cram it down so no one else could detect it. Then, it manifested as anxiety and a voracious eating disorder that damaged my heart over the course of three decades. I learned to doubt myself, my intelligence, my personality, my worthiness of being loved, my parenting, my value as a partner in a relation-ship, and my ability to stand up for myself even in the face of mistreatment. I learned how to overreact, overanalyze, and run. I learned people use you for their own benefit and that they make excuses for your feelings so they will feel better about themselves and their limitations. I learned to lie when people would ask me how I was doing. I learned I had the sharpest tongue and the quickest wit, and I often used these methods to cope because self-deprecation was easier than healing.

I didn't want to write this part of the book. I only did it because you need a road-tested guide you can learn from to achieve more in your life. I shared parts of my story because when you take a stance of trying to help people and being compassionate and empathetic, you have to offer pieces of yourself so people know where you came from. Stories have power, including yours.

My entire Facebook newsfeed resembles a litany of life coaches who have customized their training and mantras just for me. Today, I read a post from Ryan Stewman, a person I have decreed to be my living brother. He advised that people should write about all the bad stuff that's ever happened and then write down the positive life lessons from those experiences. I know well my road may have been a bit more painful than your garden-variety. But my road was necessary.

From having a scarcity of groceries and a lack of, what I felt was, safe food, that wasn't expired, or wouldn't make me sick, (and sometimes, this sickness was in my head, I know), I developed an eating disorder, and I put many rules into place to feel secure because I had never learned effective self-care.

From moving 14 times before I was 20 years old, I learned to dread change, but also learned that change was inevitable even though I hated it. I knew how to do it. Still, this is why I don't ever want to move from my home. "Home" has an almost fathomless meaning to me.

From growing up with a furious father, I learned how to be a peacekeeper. I internalized what I believed were truths about relationships and thought there should never be conflict. When there was conflict in my relationships and in my prior marriages, I did everything I could to incinerate them, so they could never be resuscitated.

From repeated abandonment stemming from a lack of emotional tools from certain relatives and friends, I learned that people do move on and that they can be dead to you even while they are still living.

This is not to say we need to focus only on positive outcomes or potentials, even though every situation contains a gift. No, we need to feel our emotions and process them to move through to an authentic end. Meaning, we must acknowledge our feelings and work through them as we honor our vulnerabilities and move forward. We must be authentic about how we receive our feelings. It is OK to have them, and it is OK to even struggle with them. We are being true to the self-nurturing we need when we get real about what we require to heal. If we deny ourselves the ability to fully grieve, get angry, and indulge in whatever emotions we need to, we are denying ourselves closure.

From overcoming an eating disorder, I've learned I can help other people. I can speak the language of fellow sufferers, and I know the habits of breaking the rules and establishing new ones to stay safe. I learned anxiety programs truths into our minds that are lies. And I learned a super effective methodology for tackling any of these old and deceitful beliefs. This method requires one step: Just do it and think about the impact of your decision later. If I had decided I wasn't going to eat a particular meat, instead of weighing the implications of what would happen if I broke my rule, I would sink my teeth into that hamburger. If I felt sick later, I would deal with it then. I had been through sickness before and survived, and I sure as hell was going to do it again. At my sickest, I was a feather on the scale at 93 lbs. and saw three different specialists between six and nine times a week to fulfill an agreement I had made with the eating disorder clinic to not be admitted as an in-patient.

I am a survivor. I am sensitive to changing my environment, probably overly so. My life has taught me that I am a person who operates magnificently from guttural levels of grit and instinct. I know how to work; I know how to wring blood out of the budget. I know how to leverage circumstances to take care of my children. I'm proud of these skills, and I offer them to other people in the forms of coaching and encouragement.

I learned anger is actually not anger; it's almost not a real thing. Rather, anger identifies a perceived threat. It feeds on the fear of this threat. This is a primal response, and when we try to have a productive conversation, anger doesn't serve us. Anger alerts you when you feel threatened or sad. Anger is the absolute definition of ego. *How dare somebody do, say, take that action toward me?* But it's all about them. Their reaction has nothing to do with us. It's about how we are perceiving what they're saying to us, which can be lost in translation through email, text, or a Facebook post. The fact is: We take our perception as truth. Meaning, if somebody says something to me, I don't reply, "Can you please define this for me? I'm very confused about what you just said." We believe what people say, but we assign meaning to their tone, expression, and body language; because of that, sometimes we misinterpret their message and assume people mean to hurt us. It's useful to think of people as bumblers. We are trying to mitigate the situation and to respond correctly under pressure and to know always what to do. That's not fair to us. That's not a healthy expectation to put on ourselves. We can identify anger, and we can also realize our anger has nothing to do with us.

Decades of counseling taught me about living with anger and abandonment, and about rewriting the rules about myself. I had to undo my tendency to be a peacekeeper and grasp the courage to stand up for my feelings in all my relationships.

This book could be too long if I talked about the impact my father's mental illness had on me, how it had left me wondering about his intentions with me. I know now, the people who love you the most can also teach you conditional love, and you will believe what they say and don't say and what they do and don't do because we assign a heavy weight to the people who are closest to us. We give them the most credence and validation…even more than we give ourselves. I don't have any ill will toward anyone, but I believe I need to share my life circumstances because they are relevant. You need to know if I am talking to you about how to be a survivor, that I chose to be one and you can too.

I have gone back and forth with a few relatives and didn't care who I hurt when I was hurting and when I felt like no one would've given a damn if I spoke up. I didn't recognize every party needs to take responsibility for their choices. I took on the burden of being the reason breakups of any sort happened and blamed myself for everything. I asked myself, *If the people who are supposed to love me the most don't, then how can anyone?* I also told myself, I was simply one of the unlucky ones and some people don't get to have families.

Therapy brought me to the point where I could make decisions to protect myself, even if it meant being with a family of my choosing. My kids taught me unconditional love, and I am forever grateful for them. My husband hung in the trenches with me even when my panic was so high that all I could do was react. He and I learned to fight together in a way where we didn't claw at each other's souls. We worked for the relationship we wanted. No amount of justifying hurtful language or behavior or betrayal should exist. The "we" comes first and the understanding and the accepted message is: "You are loved."

When you have a crappy story to tell, you have the right to tell it. You own it, and in my case, I am tired of pretending everything was OK. It wasn't. It was jacked up, and I lived through many, many moments that skewed my truth and perception of what was and would be. I needed to strip away every element dysfunction had taught me.

Surviving dysfunction and realizing you were abused on many levels is painful and hard to accept. But, this in no way diminishes you. You get to stand in your truth. Yes, our truths are ugly, but we own them, and we can't change them. You get to say, "This is what happened, and this was my part in it." I am not proud of the jabs I sent out to people who were getting too close or who hurt me, but they happened. I will not pretend for the sake of another's comfort that my story is different. I will not sugarcoat it or make it more tolerable.

We need to own ourselves and refuse to take responsibility for others. We can identify what triggers us and realize as we walk toward such sensitive pain that triggers have the potential to heal us and to heal others as well. Transforming your pain into purpose invites you into the story we all live and share. We are going to feel pain. We are going to have memories that plague us with their agonizing vividness, but we also have the choice to decide how much pain we will feel, how deep in the past we want to go, and whether we are tired of living there because our misshapen values do not serve us nor allow us to grow and prosper.

I glossed over some parts out of a consideration for length. But I own every single part of my story, and I run from nothing. I don't care what you dig up, I will talk about it. Accepting and loving myself means existing in harmony with who I was and am, including my past, present, and future.

I will share with you how I learned I was chronically ill in a later part of the book. This section was intended to be the backstory behind what got me to the point where I needed to heal, where I was sure my decisions were condemning me to more pain. If this is you and you need to start trusting somewhere and you can't even trust yourself, begin with knowing what happens in your gut when you make a wrong choice. Can you sense your gut rolling? You've made the wrong decision. When you feel dread, it's confirmation you need to do something different. Start there and build yourself into a person able to trust themselves with major decisions.

Every day, I try and remain open to what the universe will teach. I hope you will do the same as you continue to read this book. Reserve judgment, suspend preformed values, and ingest my story to help you as you live yours. I was put here on Earth to help people understand the strength of their survival skills, and I challenge myself to do the same each day. I learned to reserve my opinion as I take in new information.

This is why I work in the business of telling stories. Because when we share every bit of who we are and who we have been, we become stronger. We even begin to step into a new reality, one where we have healed and where we begin to grow whole again.

Section Two

YOUR PRESCRIPTIONS FOR TURNING PAIN INTO PURPOSE AND PROFIT

Chapter 4

WHY TRIGGERS ARE THE PATH TO PROSPERITY

We can live in harmony with our past as if the pain is part of another's story: aware of it, but still able to move forward.

Let's just put it out there already. Triggers are scary. We are taught to run from pain and not toward it. The mere word "trigger" is ahem…triggering.

A couple of weeks ago, I was paging through Spacebook, (dubbed so because it makes us all space cadets), and I came across a meme my friend, Mat Bodhi Bryan, had shared:

"Let the triggers be your guide."

It was a bolt into my heart and head. I have both gravitated toward triggers and run shrieking from them, haunted, as we all are, by their very signature meaning for us. Afraid that what we come closer to will be true. *I will learn I am disposable. I will learn I am not unique or memorable. I will learn my footprint on this Earth means nothing, that everyone who has ever wronged me was right. I will learn I am worthy of abuse.* And on it goes, the inanity filling up your core, whispering vicious secrets about you that aren't true.

Instead, what happens when we venture forward, when we poke that stick into the hole where the bees live, is that we start to understand how wrong our misperceptions are. We begin to unfurl the hurt part of ourselves, the limb we have curled into our chests that we favor tenderly. Blood starts to flow to that part of the body, yes, altered forever, but in some ways stronger.

Triggers are obstacles we can desensitize ourselves to on the way to growth.

Over and over again, we can talk about them, share the benefit of accepting them in our hearts, so that the agony of experience loses strength. It flows out of us, diluted, and as it does, we find our power.

We can live in harmony with our past, aware of what it was, without overwhelming pain. We can talk about it without crying and recite specific stories almost as if they belong to someone else. We can recognize that path to pain is as strong as we make it. We can even turn it into a twig that snaps when we put our boot on it.

Mat tells me this is a common quote used when people are healing, that triggers can equal pain and contention until they are addressed. When we do this, when we confront and sit with the agony of our triggers, we can reach pinnacles in recovery. We can turn our exposure to them from pain management to pain awareness and then begin a true healing journey.

The great news about triggers? They can launch you into new awakenings if you let them.

When you propel yourself smack into that phase, miraculous events happen.

We make different choices that have nothing to do with our past and pain.

We stop identifying ourselves as evolving out of anguish and victimization.

We become who we are supposed to be.

Tell yourself you are not:

- Incapable of working toward your passions

- The black sheep of your family

- A source of shame

- Hopeless in your relationships

- A waste of time

- Unlucky

- High maintenance

- Doomed to repeat history

- A head case

- A drama king or queen

We are our every potential. We are limitless and fascinating. We are brave enough to confront the lies that have
made up the suffering in our lives. We are in control of how
much we stand in misery.

Triggers are the keys we have been seeking to unlock
every door that has ever slammed shut in our faces. When
you wince at reading the word, you know you are there.
Acknowledge the first thought that rises from it and dig
your heels in as the pain rushes through you. What is it
telling you?

First the falsehoods. They'll wash over you like acid. Then
the cleansing, the reliving of the pain. Feel the hurt. Try not

to judge yourself for feeling it. Own your part if you have any. Forgive yourself if you need to.

Let go...

* The lies about living a worthy life. You are already worthy.

* The lies about success. You will be successful when you believe you will be.

* The lies about your capabilities and intelligence. You can become anything.

* The lies about not deserving love because of someone else's treatment of you. You deserve all the love in the world despite your past abuse or neglect.

* The lies about attaining a financially stable, stress-free life. You are not preprogrammed to fail.

Every topic that affects us can be traced back to triggers, back to the fear of re-experiencing the darkest memories, and so we run. We run from opportunity because to confront it and engage, with the potential of not meeting our aims, would validate our lies. It's too big a risk. But we go there... again and again. We seek the pain, our eyes wide, hearts hammering, our bodies unable to resist the pull. We want to understand the cause, to assign a reason for it. To learn what we did to deserve it so we can validate it and make it normal. But it will never be resolved. Not fully. Remember, deliberate pain inflicted by another makes them abnormal, not you!

Greater resolution comes from release. Mourn your attachment to pain. You will feel it as you stride into the new you. It's a scary, irreplaceable sensation. You will be OK.

Greater resolution comes from acceptance that some things have nothing to do with you. That sometimes, people are bastards who think they can exploit your emotions and heart…until they can't anymore. Because you stop them. Because you put their every action and word back on THEM.

One meme stopped me, made me curious. I gave myself over to it as I read the words for the first time 13 days ago, and having been in the trenches with my deep pain for decades, I was able to surrender. I practiced walking toward it with my arms outstretched. One meme, a few minutes to reach out to my friend and have a discussion about triggers to learn what he is doing in his life to serve others, so their memories won't turn into a personalized torture chamber anymore.

Mat Bodhi Bryan is a healer who leads from his heart source, "helping men reconnect with the divine/sacred masculine energy, healing them through creating brotherhood and setting them on the path to stepping out of society's paths, and forward into the loving masculine energy that is needed right now."

His life's work is understanding pain and moving past management into rehabilitation. Pain that is a river flowing into each nook and cranny of scar tissue we clench onto in our bodies. Let's make peace with that pain and move into prosperity in our relationships, our parenting, our businesses, our finances, our confidence.

The next time you encounter a trigger, try to resist your visceral response.

Take a moment to understand your feelings as if you were a hiker who happened to stumble across a rock with sharp edges. Regard it as much as you can without the attachment to your personal history…let it simply live in your space as you breathe through its close proximity. Then purposefully push it from your mind and rend it powerless; let your healing begin as your path to emotional wealth appears, as your path to everything you have ever hoped for finds you.

After decades of pain, I am living this. I am not a counselor, not a speaker. I am none of those things. I am just trying to live an unobtrusive existence as we all are. This is what worked for me. My healing and heart-centered resurgence of my goodness is why I share it with you.

You CAN heal. You can remove triggers, habits, and untruths about yourself to find a new path that has simply become overgrown by the pain of your past.

I hope you do. I am rooting for you.

Chapter 5

THE SECRET TO LIVING LIKE AN ABUNDANCE MAGNET

Manifesting your deepest desires and living abundantly are deliberate actions you absolutely can control.

Half of you will hate this message. Because roughly half will be the pessimistic thinkers who believe that they are not participants in their own life. The glass-half-empty peeps will perhaps want to know the secret to unlocking the door that blocks the riches from pouring in. But I decry that.

Living and cashing in mentally, physically, emotionally on an abundance mind-set is intentional; worse (sarcasm duly noted), it requires you to have a deep immovable faith in yourself.

You will not get there if you have internal work to do, if you are blaming others for your downfalls and supposed "bad luck" in life. You won't get there if your tendency is to hide in a corner and lick your wounds.

I don't say this to shame you. I share these thoughts to shine a light on the tools you need to arrive.

Living like a magnet means there is absolutely, 100 percent, zero doubt that gifts will come to you. It is sitting down and writing out exactly what you need. It is thanking the universe, the attraction force in your life, the energy bringing you the ability to take care of yourself and your family, before it arrives. This is how deliberate you are… you want no mistakes in what you are asking for, like that old joke of the dude making a wish for a thousand bucks and then peering out his window to see his yard crawling with deer.

It means knowing how to ask and being aware enough to be still. To listen and pay attention to the signs the world is sending you, that people who are part of your mission are giving to you. It is remembering when those opportunities come along to say "YES!" even if they are delivered to you in an unrecognizable manner. Even if they are not exactly what you conjured. It is being grounded enough to follow the good energy and to fine-tune what your gut is telling you or yelling at you.

When I became a full-time entrepreneur, yes, there were lean months, but the difference of being in the midst of the abundance mind-set was I never doubted the money or the jobs would be there. This was also tied to the fact I knew I was doing what I was supposed to be doing every day:

- Not sitting back and waiting for the golden illumination to come to me, not hoping to spot the searchlight shining in the fog. Instead, networking. Asking people who look like they would be a fabulous and strategic addition to my inner circle to collaborate. You should be watching for postings in FB groups, on LinkedIn; you should be writing emails to contacts. Someone once told me that we all know 250 people. Those are the people to inform of your new venture. Zone in on the people you want to speak to who feel like a solid and <u>positive connection</u>.

- Asking. I can't underscore this enough. When you meet people, ask them for what you need. Hearing "no" is OK. Hearing "no" is a reinforcement that this is not your project, not this time. Hearing "no" means it is time to approach another door, the one concealing your opportunity from you.

- Experimenting. In the beginning, as you are just getting started, it's OK to not have a completely clear direction. You will need to try a few different concentrations for the sole purpose of finding out what you are good at.

- Being still in chaos. Try to resist the urge to panic; know that you are going to be taken care of. This is the time to shut out the noise, to further distill your vision, and then to examine what is before you to see if it would be a fit. Remember that phone call about the referral prospect? Have you followed up on it? Have you, with intention pulsing plainly in your heart, gone through your usual stomping grounds, totally convinced you will find what you are looking for? I cannot tell you the number of times simply opening my mind to welcoming in blessings has changed my life and my income.

- Returning the favor. This is key to the machinations of the universe. You truly do get what you put into the world. If you are bogarting all the jobs and not demonstrating your thankfulness through reciprocation, you are missing the point. You are not defining your role of how you want to operate in the professional world. You want to accept positions, but you also want to be instrumental in helping others to reach their dreams by sharing the good fortune.

This will not work overnight, but it will work as you put it into <u>practice</u>. Sure, a huge part of this whole process is going through the motions and receiving the gifts, so you feel you are steering your course. You are. You are operating at higher vibrations. But let's not discount what each validation means. It tells you repeatedly that you are in the correct place, and this confirmation allows you to keep going confidently, which is influential in how you speak to people and how you pitch and seal deals.

When you feel you are in the right place, answering the call, snug in the hip pocket of the universe, you will act accordingly, and the more that you do, the stronger you get. It will even become challenging to pull back from your newfound power, which, at the base, is you simply and finally believing in yourself.

Before you embark on implementing the abundance mind-set, be sure to take self-inventory. Are you doing things for yourself? Are you unafraid to look at your vulnerabilities and the areas where you can improve? Are you striving to run your business unemotionally? Are you able to detach yourself from others' opinions about you? Are you strong enough to look back on your past missteps and forgive yourself without undue guilt? It is only when you believe you are a solid and good force in this world that you will succeed in unleashing the abundance mind-set, that you will begin to realize the unbelievable benefits of living like a magnet.

Chapter 6

IS REJECTION WORSE THAN FAILURE?

Rejection originates from outside forces, while allowing failure to happen comes from the inside.

It was 2002, and I was in Hollywood at Paramount Pictures, ready to read for a new sitcom on NBC. My marriage was on the rocks. I had been flown out by my agents on their dime and set up in a hotel on Sunset Boulevard. I lived with my great aunt for six weeks shortly after and drove the 2.5 hours to LA as often as I needed, committed to landing the role and any other acting jobs I could snap up that summer. I took the infamous improv Groundlings class and was shuttled into the remedial comedy sector, which I find highly amusing now. I snagged a Hollywood agent, and things were blossoming for me.

Then I bombed the audition. I played it too Midwestern, and even writing about it makes me cringe. But instead of tucking my tail between my legs, I learned about myself.

I liked being a mom more than I liked pursuing fame.

I loved writing more than acting in ridiculous scenarios.

I forgave myself for my nerves and the subsequent rejection of the producer.

My internal reasoning, *Maybe I'll be able to hit on him*, was flawed. He was one million percent gay.

No, I'm not famous, but that experience put to rest a quest to want to be more, to be loved for reasons I didn't understand. I wanted adoration from anywhere since I sure as shit hadn't subscribed to any form of self-love and didn't believe anyone else could love me either.

I wanted validation, attention, to feel like I had found my purpose. I endured finding out the opposite, and it has shaped me into who I am now.

I can take rejection. I can turn it around and pluck out the lessons I am supposed to use.

Turn here. Follow this path. Unpack this suitcase.

Rejection helped me succeed in my purpose.

I do what I love to do every single day. Write. Help people share their messages and their missions. And I am constantly in the company of the most inspiring and resilient people on the planet.

That rejection was my reboot, and it has brought me tremendous fulfillment. I had no idea what would come; I just tried to remain open to incoming knowledge.

So, is failure worse than rejection, in that situation, in any situation?

I realize this is a layered question because failure can come as a result of rejection.

You don't fail unless you accept failure. Failure means stopping progress; it doesn't mean changing your plans to achieve the same sought-after, original goal. It means reassessing if the original goal is best for you after all. Sitting in the moment when what you had dreamed about zigs instead of zags. Then after all that, deciding to bag it.

Failure is a moment in time when it all comes crashing down around you; it is a milestone of ceasing. Rejection is the return serve of your brainstorming, your pitch, your proposal, your efforts. It is the sound answer that this is not the path for you and the invitation to try again. Think of rejection like a detour sign, that there is a smoother path awaiting you. When you experience that event, then you receive invaluable information, even if that information only winds up being the fact of what *not* to do. I don't know about you, but I LOVE a little insider information.

Rejection hurts because it means you are not heard or taken seriously. As you are letting the "bad" news sink in, it feels like you have been shunned. You might feel foolish and gun-shy all at the same time; this is not fertile ground for new ideas to prosper. You must accept the rejection, but in a way that doesn't cripple you. In a way that benefits you in the future and even in the present. How can you let the new information change you for the better? My Hollywood rejection answered the questions I had about my career.

I used it to get clear. You can use your rejections, too.

We must remember rejection originates from external forces.

Failure's roots take hold on the inside.

Failure thrives on the messages we tell ourselves. That we can't do it. That we are silly, untalented, and wasting time. Failure is the brake applied as you careen through a stop sign. It is the screeching sound of momentum grinding to an immediate halt. And the aftermath of hopelessness.

Failure occurs because we let it. Because we believe in the nonsensical bullying we dream up in our heads. Because abandoning the dream is safer, hurts less. Nothing is wagered so nothing can be lost. Whew! *That was close. Right?*

Failure is easier to embrace than trying again.

Because we can pepper all sorts of validation over failure. We can bury it in platitudes and excuses not to give it another shot...using different tactics...that might just work.

The road to self-sustainable businesses is littered with potholes. And this is a fact you need to absorb so that you can learn to live with any eventuality. You will not advance down that rutted street if you stay frozen on the pavement listening to your self-limiting voice. If you want to grow, stretch, and scale, prepare for your blueprints to be rewritten a few times. Armor up emotionally to get past the vulnerable patches, and forge ahead primed to defend yourself from the blows.

Maybe we should rehearse receiving rejection.

Consider asking yourself these questions:

1. How invested was I in the turnout?

2. What lesson can I take from it?

3. How can this make me better in the future?

4. What other opportunities can come from this situation?

5. Can I understand the reason for the rejection?

Maybe we should vow to never fail whenever we can. Because to fail or not *is* in our control.

If we adopted these mind-sets, we could look back on our accelerated progress in awe of our own power and our abilities to evolve to reach our loftiest goals.

I see it happen every day. There's no reason it can't happen for you, too.

Chapter 7

IF YOU ARE A SICK OR DISABLED ENTREPRENEUR STRUGGLING TO LAUNCH YOUR BUSINESS...OPEN YOUR DOORS ANYWAY

Everyone is fighting a battle. Even if you must wear your condition like a twisted badge, unable to be hidden, start your business anyway.

According to *Inc.,* in 2015, the US was home to an estimated 27 million entrepreneurs.[1]

Statistical reports concerning the chronically ill, both in terms of the numbers affected and the severity of symptoms, are staggering.

This suggests one hell of an overlap quite a few of us entrepreneurs will fall into.

---

1. Leigh Buchanan, "The U.S. Now Has 27 Million Entrepreneurs," *Inc.*, September 2, 2015, https://www.inc.com/leigh-buchanan/us-entrepreneurship-reaches-record-highs.html?cid=search.

A peek into the state of sick self-starters reveals a slew of us do indeed battle relentless physical and mental disorders. We entrepreneurs who live and work with chronic afflictions are as ever-present as unwelcome coworkers.

Which leads me to my point.

Yesterday, I stumbled across a meme stating in stark type that in order to run a business, you must first possess perfect physical health.

Many entrepreneurs aren't blessed with flawless vitality. I'd contend that there are far more of us who are actually striving to survive a myriad of illnesses, some evident and some more invisible than might be apparent through observation or statistics. Disabilities and challenges run the gamut from physical afflictions to emotional conditions, from learning disorders to those ailments still undiagnosed. These hurdles are real and restraining, even if they aren't understood. Diabetes, Loeys-Dietz syndrome, Epstein-Barr, depression, or the disease I contend with: transverse myelitis.

So many of us are handed a life sentence, yet scores of entrepreneurs continue to conquer in the midst of misery.

It might be more accurate to assert that ill self-made men and women actually count on the rewards they receive when they plow through impasses that we may even require such "distractions" to take our minds off sustained suffering.

Medications prescribed to halt tremors, to strengthen balance and still vertigo, are not 100 percent effective. Chemo drugs may tarnish a patient's longing to work for themselves, but they don't erase it. How well a person succeeds has everything to do with their mind-set over their (perceived) sense of physical control, which is not to deny that certain diseases are more challenging to manage than others and that sometimes even the most glorious optimism may not quiet physical agony.

Your health doesn't need to be impeccable before you launch your business nor does it need to be spotless to successfully grow and sustain it.

While struggling mightily with mine—some days I would lie down and type because I didn't have the energy to sit up—I refused to be held back as I used the transformative power of positive thought to embark on a journey of reinvention even when my body called in sick. After I lost my job due to my illness, I launched into entrepreneurship out of necessity. Networked, self-taught, offered, asked, and bartered. My bar was low: achieve one goal per day. No less laudable than landing a six-figure, signed contract.

When I obtained my personal definition of victory, it was fuel to climb onto the next step.

Because the power of the mind improves the state of our life. Especially if you are an entrepreneur.

None of us will ever reach perfection in anything we do. Even if our physique qualifies us as the Eighth Wonder of the World.

Isn't that why entrepreneurs keep reaching anyway? Because that's what we are programmed to do? To slam a cap on our excitement and potential, on our very DNA, is devastating. So many of us are propelled to forge ahead, we may not have any control over stopping. The drive that resides in any one person to overcome, innovate, and create is no less intense when housed in a physically challenged body.

Recently, I partnered with several, ingenious, fertile minds, and I did it in less-than-ideal health. Because chronically ill entrepreneurs are the poster children for: "Work smarter, not harder." I needed capable and strong team members to help me be my best in business. I needed to identify work-arounds that would permit me to thrive.

To keep moving forward even as we grapple with contentious illness, we have to carefully assess the sources from which we draw advice.

If you are part of the 50 percent of the American population who has a chronic illness, it may serve you better to consider epiphanies from a person who has been in similar shoes, instead of one insisting we must achieve the impossible before we can even get started! It is dangerous to paint entrepreneurs with a broad brush and adopt the notion that you must first accomplish pristine physical health before you embark on what makes your heart sing. Plying your passion heals you! As your pulse beats bolder, as you receive recognition for your progress, you will believe it is possible to surmount the seemingly insurmountable.

Precisely the fuel you need to scale your next mountain... or business!

An excellent reason to tap into your purpose of service.

Everyone is fighting a battle. Some are better at hiding it due to the nature of their illness. Others do not have a choice and must wear their condition out loud.

You are not your disease. You have a disease. This is the singular most important truth you, as a wounded member of working society, will read.

It may require untapped innovation to keep producing. But as legions before us have proven, it is possible, and when our unique brand of victory is attained, it's breathtakingly rewarding.

Chapter 8

HOW AND WHY TO PRACTICE SENDING LOVE TO YOUR ENEMIES

You can strengthen your emotional power as you practice compassion. It's not easy, but it's freeing.

Let's start by defining what makes a person or entity an enemy. *We* assign them that label. When I impart the truth that we have the control, some seem to think that implies we prolong the pain and the venom. What I mean by that is we have control over our pronouncements and we have control over the level of pain that we will accept from others. It goes without saying that continually instigating drama or feeding into it by reacting means you will receive more pain or "venom."

I am not saying, *Well, you are causing this ongoing cycle of obsessive hatred...*but that is the reality, isn't it?

I am saying, *Realize you are in control and you get to decide your course of action. (One of my fave actions to take is to DO NOTHING.)* Because you are steering the boat, you are in charge of the suffering you allow.

That's an iron-clad position of power.

That's true empowerment. That is taming your emotions to work for you.

But, to me, it's even better than empowerment. It's building compassion.

We have the opportunity to realize, honor, and practice compassion when we are faced with the worst and most offensive behavior of humanity.

Our first reaction is understandably to take offense and protect ourselves. This is one of the strongest emotional tidal waves that can influence your behavior.

So…feel it. But try not to say anything. If you retort or respond, you influence the dynamic of the interaction. When you contribute nothing to what you know will be a useless fight, then the actions of the other person remain in the light. *Because you have not used your tongue or body language to make it worse.*

You don't want to deny yourself the right to work through any emotion. The way our bodies receive information is instinctual; so seriously, I just allow it to happen. If I need to, I try to use the time when I am not reacting to calm down.

Not engaging has saved me so much pain and adrenaline coursing through my body. It has kept my health in better check and given me more peace. *I like myself better when I don't get all tangled up and nasty.* Studies have shown the continual dumping of stress-induced cortisol into our bodies can lead to chronic illness. I believe my body finally broke after so much emotional tumult.

It takes a long time for wounds to heal. It seems like we get the physical part of healing confused with the emotional part of healing. A punch to the face resulting in a black eye will heal far faster than a wound to your very core.

Every time we take an action or say something in relation to conflict, we reopen the wound. Holy moly, I did that for *years*.

Now, I realize I have a choice, and with it came four other realizations:

1. Conflict is normal.

2. Conflict is not something to be afraid of. (I still use self-soothing mantras to reinforce this.)

3. A perfectly acceptable response is not to say or do anything.

4. I can up the ante on no. 3, and in addition, meditate on what suffering is plaguing my enemy.

This new realization came about when I read the book *The Shack*. It's not that I hadn't heard of the concept and power of forgiveness, but I was stuck. I wanted to forgive, but I wouldn't allow myself. Some part of me still hadn't gotten what I thought I had coming, and I wanted to stick around and feel miserable in the conflict *because it made me feel important.*

That is absolutely the wrong reason to prolong pain. That is what professionals call negative reinforcement.

I bawled when I read *The Shack*. Cried as silently as I could as I watched the movie, sitting next to my husband who was sleeping. I literally went through a half a box of tissues one late night.

I said, "I forgive you, (insert name)." Then I let it roar in my heart. I could nearly feel the stitching of the needle and thread sewing me back together. I wept. Because I had acknowledged I had been hurt by recognizing a need to forgive, I had to finally weep. I had to mourn my pain a few final times. Hence, the half a box of tissues. On it went for a couple more days. I was tender.

But the light came on.

I could see people lashing out because of their own pain.

Because of fear. (Anger is a poor disguise for fear.)

Because of sadness and hurt.

I started sending them love instead of raw fury. I started taking myself out of their picture (how presumptuous of me, anyway!) and seeing that they alone hold their memories and their misery, regardless of my existence. Disentangling my emotional weight from theirs allowed me to rise out of the agony I had dwelt in for so long.

Let me tell you…

- Someone else's addiction is not your issue.

- Someone else's inability to manage their anger is not your problem to solve.

- Someone else's pain impasses aren't yours.

- Their judgment is not your burden.

- Their fear is not your battle.

- Their self-loathing obstacles are not your job to remove.

You are in a better place when you can compartmentalize suffering. You can be objective and choose to retain your own health.

And when you do, you can start to wish for the pain of others to lift *from them.*

Such pain is a terrible load to carry. Aren't you lucky you aren't hauling that around?

I have flipped the script on hatred, and now I send loving messages on the wind...

I wish you well.

I wish you to love yourself.

I wish you success.

I wish you joy.

I wish you to stop blaming yourself.

I wish you to see yourself for your amazing gifts.

I wish you to know it's not too late.

I wish you would see no one is as hard on you as you are on yourself.

Selfishly? You will feel so much better about yourself as you strive to reach the pinnacle of being the best person you can be, as you fill your heart with what makes you feel wonderful...doing good and spreading around the warm echoes of your heart.

It is so helpful to remember that a huge percentage of the time, a person's reactions and words have nothing to do with you. There are outside and inside influences of which you are not aware.

It took me decades to get here. I hope this chapter will give you a little jump-start so you don't have to wait so long to plant the buds of inner peace.

Chapter 9

FIVE WAYS TO DEFINE YOUR SELF-WORTH IN AND OUT OF THE OFFICE

You can take a hit and emerge intact. Stronger, even.

You might have read the title of this chapter and thought to yourself, *I don't need any help defining my worth. I know I'm awesome*! This is fabulous news for you, but many people struggle with feeling <u>worthwhile</u>, and that is why I am writing.

I have a friend who creates striking artwork, all sorts of products that draw in your eye with their vivid colors and patterns. Since she is just starting, her sales are a bit anemic. It's hitting her confidence, and it makes me sad. I wish I could convince her that she should keep at it. That the lack of dollars flowing in is not a reflection of her work. (I know because I don't have bad taste.) She simply hasn't found her niche nor her buyers yet.

Guess how long I've been writing professionally? In earnest, I began pouring my attention into my business about two and a half years ago, when I became a writer for *The Good*

Men Project. I did not wake up overnight and find that *Huffington* had handed me a blogger account, or that my optimal clients were lined up and ready to give me cash. I had to work at it. Consistently. Tirelessly. Through owning my triumphs and doubts. The journey needed to remain the same, despite the veers and swerves coming at me.

Through it all, I maintained my self-worth, even after I had taken a beating (a few times).

Baptism by fire.

So, if you are embarking on a start-up, working in a career you love in a company owned by another, or just can't seem to shake disappointment within yourself, when you read these points and apply them, they will help.

1. **Objectivity**—It is paramount to learn and practice this skill of delineating one event from the next. Not everything is related. Because you lost a client doesn't mean suddenly your talents have disappeared. It might be as simple as your client going through rocky financial times, or sometimes, your vision doesn't jive…but that doesn't mean you are untalented, should hang up your paintbrushes, your laptop, or other implements that define you. It means you have a differing point of view, but not a wrong one.

2. **Remember your successes**—How did you feel after a landslide win? Pretty empowered probably. Have you

stopped to think about what facilitated that win? Have you examined the clients with whom you work best? If you are struggling to close deals and sign new clients, take a step back and examine your strengths, the things that you absolutely rock at doing. The niches where you soar. The deals that are easy to sign and that effortlessly find their way to you…that is where you want to concentrate. This is why people choose a specialty and work on it for *years*. This is putting in the time to find out where you should apply your efforts.

3. **You deserve self-worth because you are a person—** Period. Listen, even when you stumble, even in your moments where you aren't feeling so proud, it doesn't take away from the fact that you should feel good about your efforts. Maybe that doesn't put money on the table, but this is a part of life and business. You are going to fail, and it is up to you to be kind to yourself *when* it happens. Yes, learn from it. Take the lesson in. But do not berate yourself when a slip happens after you have tried your hardest.

4. **Resilience—**I am not telling you to suck it up, but I am saying that you are more powerful than you think. You will feel as bad about yourself as you allow. If you want to feel like crap for an hour, a day, a week, this is all in your hands. So is feeling awesome about yourself and the mission you undertake every day. Are you going to fight when you feel bad, or are you going to succumb to (let's face it) what is easier, giving up? It takes guts and mettle to

continually put yourself and your ideas out there when you could potentially be shredded by your boss, a prospective client, or even a friend. If you want to get better, learn to pluck out the helpful critique and throw the rest on the ash heap. Which leads me to my next point.

5. **Selective Critique**—When people are coming at you with suggestions, or you are receiving lukewarm reviews, remember this: Stand by your decision, but allow yourself to hear the useful feedback. This is a tricky art. Let me give you an example. When I wrote my first thriller novel, I was hungry for feedback. I wanted to get better. I dreamt of grabbing that best-selling-novelist golden ring. I squared up my emotions and attitude and dispersed it to over 60 people. The reviews came back, and they were ugly and I responded by ugly crying. But a little twinge inside me, worming around in my gut, told me what I already knew. I needed to listen, or I would never improve. So, I did. I read the reviews, thanked people for taking the time to read my material, and as I did this, I discovered not everyone has something valid to say. One person might've said, "I hate the name you gave your protagonist." And another would love it. Someone else might've written that a character seemed a little one-dimensional, and another person might've disagreed with that opinion. I couldn't please everybody and neither can you. I had to take the useful information and apply it to any changes I made. I still use this approach in my work. "I hate the color green." Well, that's super great, but if it's germane to your brand, you

better get used to it. We need to make strategic choices for improvements, and when we do this, there is nothing to defend. Because we have a solid reason for our decisions.

You have to be made of Teflon to live in this world, and you can strike the balance of feeling the sadness about loss without having it destroy you or who you are as a person. It doesn't have to call into question that you have strengths unique to you. Validation from outside sources (what we get so used to seeking from social media) isn't all it's cracked up to be. In this breakneck world, take a moment, look inward, and applaud yourself for every undertaking and for being strong enough to survive.

Chapter 10

WHY SELF-DOUBTS LEAD TO SELF-SABOTAGE IN BUSINESS

Our thoughts DO become our actions. Change your thoughts, change your life.

There are two types of people I deal with on a daily basis. The people who are positive and persistent (even their speech reflects this), and people who seem to hope for the best, but whose words trip up their chance at success.

Here's an example of conversations with two entrepreneurs:

Entrepreneur 1: Yes, I absolutely can make that work in my schedule! I just reached out to this contact, and I know we are going to hit it off. I'll have a contract by the end of the week.

Entrepreneur 2: I'll try and make it happen. It might work out, and I hope it does. I tried my hardest to close that deal, but now we just wait and see. I'll have a backup plan, just in case.

Two great people whose work I greatly respect and admire. Two people packed with talent. Two different ways of phrasing opportunities in their life.

No, not everyone can be all gung-ho and "let's move mountains." OK, I accept that, but also accept that nine times out of ten, the more cautious entrepreneur is not going to get that gold ring.

Why?

The saying, "Our thoughts become our actions," is true.

Any little crack in the armor, any minor crimp in the chain, will betray your body language and the confidence of your words.

I looked back at my Facebook timeline, and this was a fascinating exercise. I encourage you to do it.

2009

Hilary Lauren Jastram
December 19 2009

Do you ever feel like you are being dragged behind the truck called life?

Like   Comment   Share

2017, a few days ago.

What's the difference? Something snapped in me after I hit my bottom in 2009. My marriage broke up, my family took sides, my kids were miserable, I was losing my house, and I FELT LIKE A VICTIM. So, I approached my life that way... as if everything was out of my control...as if I were merely fulfilling my destiny to struggle...as if I would always be the black sheep of the family. My self-deprecating humor reflected this. Oh, I was funny AF, but I was hurting. I would make jokes at my own expense, and everyone would laugh, but I was covering up the fact that I felt like a failure, like I couldn't fit in anywhere. I had no idea what I was doing... and my feelings about my inabilities sprang into life!

I couldn't get ahead at work because I didn't believe I was ever going to be good enough.

I usually couldn't make a relationship last longer than five years because I didn't know what that kind of work entailed. I couldn't control my emotions because I believed I was a (reckless) crusader. I couldn't confidently parent my children because I second-guessed myself. I didn't believe I would ever get better or would ever recover from an eating disorder, and I thought that I would always be a disappointment and "too much" for anyone else to handle.

I wish I could tell you when I woke up. I wish I could tell you when I began to realize my job here on Earth is to encourage people and to love them into their own acceptance.

One day it changed.

Then I took that same life-changing action the next day. The more I accomplished in my head—the more that I REFUSED to make jokes about my supposed lack of worth—the more I believed it.

I reset my emotions. I looked at everything I needed to do to heal with the loving acceptance of ME. Instead of feeling shame at my past mistakes, I accepted them and did not blame my past or anyone else for them...HOWEVER, with the level of shit I was exposed to, I could UNDERSTAND my poor decisions. I loved myself into acceptance and true forgiveness.

It improved my personal life, my relationships in all areas, and my business.

Because you cannot believe that you are a worthless pile and then go on ahead and close significant deals, forge contacts, and expect to win over prospects. You have to believe you are capable in every area of your life.

FOR ONE HOUR, change your self-talk. Stop joking about how inept you are, etc. Because when you do, you are both continually trying to accept your perceived shortcomings and punishing yourself for having them. People say, "It's all in good fun. I don't really mean it about myself." But you put the thought into action in your head. You manifested the negative belief that reflects in everything you do. After one hour (be strict with yourself now because self-love is tough love), try two. And three and so on.

Watch what happens.

Events you believe to be out of your control suddenly aren't (although I recognize all we do is strive for control). I'm talking about opportunities. I'm talking about using good and healthy habits to improve your life.

Start today, and in three months look back on your Facebook timeline. As an aside, I don't need motivational coaches. My feed is filled with the most encouraging, uplifting, positive messages you could ever see or fathom. I use my newsfeed to fill my soul and reinforce my confidence. You can do the very same thing. Start unfollowing and block that draining energy!

When you change the messages you believe about yourself on the inside, you *will not believe* the impact on the outside.

Chapter 11

13 INDISPENSABLE ACTIONS CHRONICALLY ILL ENTREPRENEURS NEED TO TAKE

Mind-set is the conqueror of what ails you.

By the year 2020, close to 160 million people will live with a chronic illness, with "81 million having multiple conditions."[2] Many of those people have been forced into working for themselves. For me, it was a fortunate event—I mean, after I had gotten my disease under control. Since finding success in the entrepreneurial world, I wanted to share the tips I wish I'd known before embarking on my entrepreneurial journey, the tips that allowed me to accomplish more than I thought I could. That will help you to do the same.

How to Excel

1. **Structure your business around your needs.** Do you require time during the day to rest? Are you unable to

2. "About Chronic Diseases," National Health Council, last modified July 29, 2014, http://www.nationalhealthcouncil.org/sites/default/files/NHC_Files/Pdf_Files/AboutChronicDisease.pdf.

work on-site? What schedule works best? How many hours of sleep do you need each night? Make yourself a priority; build safety nets into your schedule and projects.

2. **Don't live in fear of your illness, and don't let illness control your business.** Use your mind instead of your body. Honor your skills and experience. Needing assistance to walk doesn't mean you need help in the innovation department, in networking, or in crushing your goals. Slaying business is a great distraction from physical distress!

3. **Don't ignore your illness.** Live consistently within a schedule. Estimate the number of hours per day you need to dedicate to work. When you do this, you invite opportunities because you will be primed and fresh! Productivity is a mind-set! If you're dedicated to results, it doesn't matter what you wear or where you are.

4. **Offer transparency to your clients.** This is the only way to do business, to work with clients compassionate to your situation. Anyone else pushing you without empathy—well, those aren't your people anyway. Disabled and ill people get a bad rap because some abuse the system. This chapter is not for them. It's for *you*. You who want to ride the wave of passion to your dreams.

5. **Know that you can say no to preserve your health and you can say no because you want to— just as anyone else would.** Boundaries are important. High achievers have a tremendously difficult time saying

no, out of fear of loss. You will not lose anything you can't recover if you refuse a project. When you need the time to recoup, *take it*!

6. **Figure out which project structure, days versus hours, suits you best, and set your work up in this way.**

7. **Remember it is not about how much you need to make; it's about what you can make.** When you approach goals from a self-limiting belief, you are predisposed to tank your chances at overcoming challenges. Imagine, instead, you are limitless, and watch your entrepreneurship open up. This is simply the art of reinvention, my friend.

8. **Plan for relapses and build your network to accommodate them.** If you know x amount of hours is going to impact you negatively, consider a schedule that incorporates working every day with fewer hours. If you know you need weekends to recharge, arrange your obligations to occur M–F.

9. **Find the gift in your disease.** Adverse events provide us with hidden opportunities; they permit our minds to experience life differently than if we were working 9–5 every day. It sounds insane, but you will discover silver linings. I have been able to write more, revel in a no-rules business, and embrace deeper relationships and a stronger self-worth.

10. **Live your business's purpose.** You get to select your professional company. Self-made people. Inspiring people with awesome missions. You'll be enveloped into their energy and their "why" and get paid, too!

11. **Don't sell yourself short because of your disease.** Know what you're worth and ask for it. Your mind is still spry. You can think. Solve. Innovate. You can do anything. Working with a person who has a chronic illness is an advantage because we have been forced to grow out of our fears and necessities. We are confident in our resourcefulness and perseverance.

12. **Use it to take you out of your world sometimes.** When I get to write, when I am strategizing, speaking to clients, and coaxing their ideas to fruition, I lose myself and I am grateful. I become part of a collaboration, and I become resilient to the inner forces trying to besiege me!

13. **Equip yourself with the right tools.** Do you need Adobe Suite, video editing software, analysis tools? Subscribe/rent/purchase the best tools in your industry so when a client asks you to do something, you won't hesitate. Nothing shuts down a prospect faster than a professional scrambling to accommodate business needs.

You have a choice if you are sick and working—hell, if you are well and working—in how you handle "hurdles." *Mind-set* can hold you back or launch you forward into the greatest success you ever imagined.

Chapter 12

HOW TO BECOME ABSOLUTE TEFLON IN BUSINESS

Take in constructive feedback meant for you that helps explode your potential. Everything else slides off your armor and hits the floor.

Growing in business requires taking chances. Taking chances requires sticking your neck out, with the possibility you will get your head chopped off. Getting your head chopped off...oh, I got ahead of myself. You can't work without a head, although some people try valiantly, but that is a topic for another time.

The point is that, in running a business, you will take missteps, you will estimate (wrongly), you will disappoint, look like an ass, say the wrong thing, and cringe when you say it.

It is not for the faint of heart.

But neither is denying your passion. Denial is a rigorous journey through hell. I would rather take my chances trying my absolute best with my intentions in the right place than surrender to fear.

Listen, you are not a robot. You are a person who weighs a stack of decisions every day. Sometimes, you venture out on that branch a little farther than you should. Me too.

The old adage is correct: "Whatever other people think of you is none of your business."

Not only is it none of your business, but it also massively holds you back because we sit and spin on an opinion which we have no control over, which we labor to understand… even though we never will because we are not the originator of the thought. We are simply the receiver.

It is our job to listen, to evaluate depth and meaning, to decide if we need to take action (if the comment lobbed our way was valuable), but it is *not our job to absorb this feedback*.

If you think about it, this act of attempted osmosis is actually selfish and presumptuous. Who are we to impact ourselves this way? Who are we to assume such a weighty statement is dedicated to us in complete totality? Who are we to lose time and momentum from our very progress and our achievements?

When we do, it affects us greatly, holds up the train, which would otherwise blaze down the track. The train of thought, the train of action, the train of positivity, and belief.

It's selfish. It affects others in our realm. It's shortsighted, gritty, arrogant. It's not for us.

We need to take in what *is* for us.

This is not to decry the need to hear feedback, to improve. There is a chasm between constructive criticism (meant to push you into robust acceleration and purpose) and trolling.

Here are a handful of mind-set mentalities to lock into:

1. **Your treatment by others is directly connected to how you treat others.** This is magnetism; this is spirit and vibration. The law of attraction. It is why, until a person does the internal work of cutting out toxic people, they can expect more of the same...no matter the area of life: personal, business, friendships, family. Treat people well. State your feelings. Resist being a peacekeeper. Own your stuff; refuse to carry others' baggage. Be kind and open and offer to help, even if it puts you out a little, even when it doesn't directly impact you. Recall also this word: humility. It's a grounding idea as well as an arrow pointing out opportunities.

2. **Picture a Teflon plate in your chest.** Think of the negativity, the unnecessary roughness (if you will), as an egg sliding off that plate and hitting the floor. Envisioning and changing your perspective holds a particular enriching power. This mind-set will take you out of feeling sorry for yourself (never a good idea when you are an entrepreneur grinding to sell yourself all. day. long.). Even if what you are hearing is relevant and helpful, even if it has been

delivered in a gentle way, do not absorb it to the point of obsession. Listen, pluck out the points that, when implemented, will improve your business, your approach, etc. And that's it. You must reinforce this barrier. This is not to discount the fact that hearing honest and seemingly harsh truths about yourself is twinge-worthy. It is. But let's not belabor the point either; let's not to fixate on it. Certainly, NEVER mold your next strategic step around another's view of how *you* should succeed. Only specific ideas and mantras should be permitted to penetrate past your Teflon. The rest are eggs on the floor.

3. **You are only as good as your trustworthy resources.** People who care about you and your business matter. Not the cage-rattlers (people who seem to cheer your success but secretly resent it), not the ones out to make a buck off you, who run your energy into the ground by demanding all your time, not respecting your calendar, etc. These people are not good wells from which to drink. We have all worked with these personalities, and when you need to hone your skill set, do not use these contacts. I don't care who you ask for an honest assessment: a spouse, friend, a coworker, a mentor. Just make sure that you seek honest information about yourself from a source you can trust.

4. **Detach from your past.** It is easier said than done but make a concerted effort to approach each interaction with a clean slate. It is supremely challenging to leave

behind our experiences as we enter into new phases of our life, but it is critical that we do so, so we can have the freshest perspective on the realities of every situation. So many times, what people say, feel, do is more a reflection of them and their experiences and not yours. Another old saying applies: "Keep your side of the street clean." When you do that, when you refute the bulk of past decisions and experiences trailing along behind you, you will have clarity of focus about the situation you're in. This also applies to relationships, FYI.

5. **Remember your victories.** When I am having a day sluggish in momentum, when I am running up against walls, it is tempting to fold. It is tempting to start the one-up internal game. But instead of devolving into a pity party, which can snowball out of control, I think about how far I have come. How fortunate I am to work in my chosen field every day. How pure determination, willingness, and an open heart have done more for me than anything else. I remember to ease up on the pressure and realize I'm having a moment where I might need a little more introspection versus hard-charging directives. I stop and let gratitude wash over me, remind myself, this, all of it, this glorious and messy life and existence is all a part of it. Every day will not be a glossy ray of hope, handed effortlessly over. We might need to work for it, to argue for the right to take action, to convince, to listen, to expand. The road will not always be rut-free. But I have navigated that road, and so have you. I have made progress

on that road. I am proving I can do this every day. Through sheer perseverance, through renewed passion, through openness to reinvention. Remember your wins. Write them down if you have to.

Some Examples of Wins

1. Closed a contract

2. Consulted on a business project

3. Was quoted on a media site

4. Expanded my team

5. Created a new service/offering

You want the life you have chosen for yourself. You deliberately plot your moves to win every day. Each day is the same and, hopefully, better. Protect yourself, your interests, and your lifeblood through the use of boundaries, detachment, and defense of your professional core.

Chapter 13

THE ONLY TWO QUESTIONS YOU NEED TO ASK BEFORE MAKING ANY DECISION

Faced with a small choice or a monumental decision, being honest with yourself about these two truths will set you off in the right direction.

Ah, life, getting in the way of everything. So complex, coloring our judgment of any decision that's got us sitting on the fence. Relationships, obligations, passion: our lives are a daily combustion chamber of choices.

We are put in touch with more people—some who should remain a mystery—and we go on, leapfrogging across the calendar from appointment to appointment, playdate to playdate, date night to date night, scratching in a message for a little affection here and there.

When we need to make a decision in the snarl of such socially acceptable chaos, how do we distill the true and best choices, ones which do not make us codependent, ones that align emotion with intention without confusing the two?

It's quite simple really. Just ask yourself these two questions—and be honest about the answers! Resist the urge to tag on any justification, and limit your answer to "yes" or "no."

1. **Will I have more good than bad days if I make this decision?**

This worked quite well for me when I had no idea if my geriatric Chihuahua needed to be put down. We had never had an aged pet in our home. Our cats had died young from rare diseases. I called the emergency vet after we had changed Bijoux's food and asked him how I would know when the time was right to end Bijoux's life peacefully. I didn't want her to suffer, and I didn't want her to die prematurely, yet I couldn't take emotion out of the equation. The vet tech responded, "Is she having more good than bad days?" And like that, the decision was made! Bijoux still danced around and didn't act as if she were in pain; her intestinal issues turned out to be minor and were remedied with another food change. We put her down a couple of years later when her physical distress could no longer be ignored.

Bijoux's experience led me to ask this question of the many pending pieces in my life: Would I have more good than bad days if I tried to return to work full time? Would we have more good than bad days if my adult child moved back in with us? Would I have more good than bad days if we bought a house for its gorgeous colonial features even though we couldn't really afford it? (Darn it!) Would I have more good than bad days if I stopped putting off a surgery? This question eliminates any doubt, any urge you may have to argue for what your gut tells you will not be good for you.

New job? Great! Less pay and a lateral move? Will you have more good than bad days? Marriage proposal? Congratulations! Before you accept, and as you realize your loved one is circling with a ring, ask yourself: Will you have more good or bad days in your marriage?

2. **How'd that work out for you last time?**

The first time I was asked this question, I became ticked off immediately because it was laced with a chuckle that made it sound as though the asker might be making fun of me. After I calmed down, I solved the reason for my ire. This question is an honest one and brings you face-to-face with the results of your life choices.

Some of my choices sucked and being reminded about my suckage stung. I laughed it off, while cringing from the blow, and then began to evaluate a handful of my toxic habits. I hadn't wanted to be alone. How had that worked out for me last time, spinning the merry wheel of mates, hoping to land on a viable catch?

I'd needed a job as a single mother, any job. How had that worked out for me after I'd subtracted passion, location, pride? Any situation is applicable, and the answers—if you are truthful with yourself—can direct you toward a happier, more profitable path in terms of your personal growth, relationships, and career. You can use it to decide about having more children, buying that couch on sale, giving the blind date a shot, whatever you apply.

Since I've synced my heart and head, I'm confident about my decisions. I speak my mind when these questions uncover a lingering doubt about any possible option, and I make sure doubts are addressed before defining a new direction. If the doubts don't go away, the decision is scrapped to be reconsidered at a later date, when the circumstances are right, and I am ready for the next step. If that day ever comes. If it doesn't, I'll still be alright, and so will you.

Chapter 14

11 STEPS TO REGAIN FAITH IN YOURSELF

In this 21st century, life is different, moving at breakneck speed; it's all we can do to keep up. As much as we try to plan the details of our lives, sometimes events happen beyond our control, or we might realize we have no control. The visions others have for their lives and personal evolutions and the hopes they have for where they wish their journey to take them, their company, or their relationship, may not play nicely with the path we have carved to lead us to the future we desire. This is survival-mode insight on how to accept your new normal, whether it be a devastating diagnosis, an unanticipated breakup, a bankruptcy, or another equally surprising occurrence, and it is your road map for getting on with your life.

When life smashes missiles over the net, similar to a relentless tennis ball blaster, and we can hardly recover before getting blasted again, it's natural for our faith in ourselves to falter. In the midst of loss of control, we get angry, and we fight and thrash to regain what we've lost.

People start in with the well-meaning platitudes: *You gotta look up. It just means something better is ahead. You're having a rough patch; you'll figure it out. Be thankful for that* other thing you have going on. All great intentions, however invalidating. What's the matter with being sad, with lingering in a woeful space and letting anger gnash you up? What's the matter with feeling? Why are we so encouraged to shake it off?

I read a friend's post expressing bald emotion over a serious injury, telling her circle she didn't want to be OK, even as she felt so much pressure to be happy, to catch the effing epiphany elevator, which would take her to the top again. She suffered a big blow, and it might change her life. I am so proud of her for defending her right to feel like crap.

When you lose faith because of a life-180, cover these bases as you implement your powerful truth: *You are OK being not OK.* In fact, you're glorious.

1. **Get into the feeling groove.** Hurl bottles at a cement wall. Crush cans. Get your hands on an old phone book and tear it apart. Compartmentalize and confine your angst to a canvas through painting. Fill a blank page with your emotional musings. If you're sad, commit to being the best pathetic lump, wallow under the covers, watch movies that play your heartstrings like a harp, listen to *"our song"* on repeat, and weep with pride and wonder. Whatever you're

feeling, welcome it into your body to wring its contents out so you can be done with it. <u>Finish your emotion</u>.

2. **Put a time limit on your grieving.** Wade in the worst of it for two days only. Anything longer and you are wasting time getting on. You need a limit so you don't live in this new, untenable space. Dwelling in the belly of sadness or fury is not living at all. If you can't move on after two weeks, please talk to a counselor or therapist who will assist you in developing your new to-dos.

3. **Understand you're not predictable.** You will feel what you are going to feel when you feel it—and not just emotionally either. Your emotions will bring with them some major physical symptoms that will have to be dealt with. The severity, frequency, and chaotic occurrence of them may surprise you. Anticipating this phenomenon helps to buffer the blow. As a panic attack sufferer, I have learned to ride that wobbly horse, to hang onto the stringy mane when I think I'll be bucked off. Even when it seems as if I'm going to die. Literally die. I chant in my head, *I am OK*. I will survive the nausea, the stomach churns, the tremors wracking my body, and I always do. Because our bodies and minds are miracles.

4. **Reassure yourself the worst isn't going to happen.** The bottom probably won't drop out in the next 24 hours. Or next week. Unless you're defending yourself from a

catastrophe of biblical or bodily proportions, ease up on the worst-case scenarios. You will rise to see the sun color the morning, you will live to survive the changes in your life, you will conquer moving on from your ex, your job, your loss of mobility, your former friend. <u>You will live to survive</u>.

5. **Trust.** When we've done everything to safeguard our future, our relationship, whatever dried up and blew away, it's very hard to trust in the future and to trust ourselves. You lose faith in yourself to do anything right, think you read signs all wrong, question if you ever knew how to gauge people. We can turn compulsive about these issues, second-guessing simple decisions. It's a very natural and an understandable defense mechanism, which wells up for one reason: to protect us. *Be cautious*, we hear our inner voice whispering, chastising our last choice. Please stop over-thinking. Please…breathe. Be in the moment. Release the need for immediate gratification, for instant knowledge of where you'll wind up. The amount of planning and obsessing you invest in your day-to-day dealings may not even matter in the scope of the larger picture. Have faith, a solution you haven't considered may be imminent.

6. **Treasure your faith.** You need it as an intangible entity reaching down to pull you up. You need it as a ray of sun behind a door. You need the light-limned cloud so you can radiate toward it. If you didn't want to live, you wouldn't, but even the crabbiest among us choose to breathe and forge ahead. You must have faith in solutions

even when you have been reduced to shreds of who you used to be.

7. Clear out toxic energy and believe in yourself. Toxic energy blocks you. Negative associations with people who manipulate, who are passive-aggressive with you until you're feeble and weak, cage rattlers, the yeah but-ters, the one-uppers, usher them all out and envision yourself in that new job. In that relationship holding hands with your dream lover as you slog through puddles. Success is 90% informed by our attitudes; the rest is connecting the dots.

8. **Write it down.** When I wanted a full-time gig at a corporation, retirement, and benefits, I wrote down my aims over and over. In cursive, typed, in block letters, on legal paper, on blank, creamy white paper, on the backs of bill envelopes. I wrote my goals down so my actions gravitated toward fulfillment. I saw my desired end result and was forced to live as if I were getting there. When I was finally confronted with the opportunity at the crossroads, I went where I was supposed to go, the finish line.

9. **Take baby steps, baby.** When you have no idea how to go, where to go, what part of the mess to clean up first, begin somewhere. That loose end? Tie it up. Make that phone call. Manage your life. Achieving baby steps will restore a greater inner faith that you can use to achieve bigger steps.

10. **Remember there are no guarantees.** It's funny, I used to think I had a right to a perfect life, to a beautiful house, to good treatment by others. My way of insuring an ideal reality was comprised of getting my poop in a scoop and waiting for the rewards to come pouring in. Realizing there are no guarantees helped sharpen my focus. I wasn't being slighted or personally targeted because I contracted a disease, lost my job, and then…my health insurance (an important detail when you have a disease)! I was, and am merely, a human cruising through life, hitting unseen hurdles just like everyone else. Our problems crop up like weeds defying extermination. Coexist with the weeds. Reroute around that sprouting abomination and walk on.

11. **Reinvent yourself now.** I regard these unknown moments as the blessing of a renaissance, and I try to resolve the reason for the change. What am I supposed to learn? The truth is the answer might be nothing, but reinvention is an ideal time to sit back and figure out the lesson…if there is one. Take advantage of the positives in your altered existence. These sweet nuggets are all yours to savor, and after what you've been through, you deserve it.

Chapter 15

HOW PRACTICING ONE SMALL HABIT CAN CHANGE YOUR LIFE

Instead of wondering why your life is so hard, change it by doing one simple thing.

Living in a rut is exhausting. You may know someone who seems unlucky, or maybe you feel that way yourself. Your inner voice echoes, *I can't believe all that's happening to me. I must be the unluckiest person alive.* Or maybe, *This isn't my day...again.*

You make plans, do your best to follow through with the details. You might overanalyze, and still you wonder, *Why in the world is my life so hard?*

I have talked to many people about their issues, especially since I've gotten chronically ill. Other members of my support group and I share symptom similarities, relate how we feel in a safe space, and I have noticed there are some who heal better, more quickly, and with a greater lasting impact than others.

The secret?

Positivity.

I don't mean disingenuous positivity, slapping on a smile you can't feel or truly don't want to wear, when you put that grin on your face to pretend you are OK. That's forced and fake. I'm talking about changing the messages you give yourself. Call it self-affirmation, if you want.

We start with internal thoughts before we voice opinions and feelings. These secret musings become words we manifest.

It's why your external change starts inside. Because when you deliver negative, discouraging missives to yourself, you are issuing a truth: *I can't do this. I can't change this.* Or, *I am a victim.*

Your unspoken thoughts become actions specifically designed to fail because you don't believe in what you are doing or what you are going after.

Swap those tacit, damaging recitations for different ones: *I can learn from this. What am I trying to accomplish? What is my gut telling me?* Separate your heart from your gut. What's good for you? Get logical with your emotions. Forget what you want. What do you *need?*

Then, focus on shoring up your confidence when you go after your goals. *I can do this. One setback is not going to keep me from my aim. Failure gives me the opportunity to learn.*

When I distanced myself from what could hurt me and stopped interpreting the intention behind words, I grew a thicker skin. People were not trying to enter my body to destroy my soul. The more I apply this mantra in my life—*I want the truth*—the more I grow, the more effective I become in my work, and the closer my relationships become. All of this is confidence fodder. When you reach this stage, you can go on feeling better about yourself and your abilities, which begins to feed into your subsequent endeavors until you have manifested a long, wondrous chain.

The next time you feel disappointment, use it as an opportunity to change your voice to that of an intentional victor. Get honest and fearless. Did things go south because the decision didn't originate from your gut? Substitute scolding yourself with regrouping and refocusing. Tell yourself, *I can do this because I say I can. I will do this because I believe I will.* You are your most credible testament. Repeat the mantra in your head as many times as you need, shut down any creeping, doubtful suggestions. Say your mantra again. *I can.* Then you will.

Chapter 16

THE TRICKY ART OF HANGING ON DURING LIFE-RATTLING EVENTS

The stress I used to think was a big deal…wasn't. Evenings after work, I would rush in the door, run to my bedroom, shuck off my work clothes, and head upstairs to make dinner. I wondered how I could continue at this insane pace as I plugged myself into my place at the dining room table and tried to decompress.

Turns out, continuing to figure it out was not to be. I got life-changing sick. The household recoiled as if forced to sit next to a pestilent, grotesque stain that had plopped itself on the couch. Mom catching a disease is a big deal, and we weathered a number of cracks in the foundation. Sure, we emerged with black eyes and broken teeth, but we emerged.

I guess I thought this illness had an end, as in, *Well, it's me, and I'm immune to death or anything which would advance my demise, so this weird little blip will be over soon.* Yet it keeps going on, and it keeps bringing new obstacles as it goes. Lost and disinterested friends. Check. Strained relationship. Check. Lost job. Check. Scared and angry kids. Check. Lapsed health insurance. Check. I could go on, but I think you get the picture.

I reinvented myself. Climbed back into my chrysalis as many times as I needed to try and re-birth myself as the right damn animal. Something fluffy and sweet with giant anime eyes, half platypus, half parakeet? I still haven't gotten it right. The illness persists.

What do you do when you are forced to change, when the process of morphing pushes you away from the people you love the most? An illness can be a deal breaker. The stark terms of your life laid out, stripped down, and disassembled force an awakening. Awakenings are usually a blessed bonus, but it's no surprise that awakenings can also drive a wedge between you and, well, everyone. Nothing is more shocking than the underbelly of disease. Sick people can have jerky personalities. Well, people can act like asses… to sick people.

So, you spend a lot of time being mad. You question, *Who am I to be angry when a perfect life is never promised? Why did I envision myself among the haughty and healthy, and do I really think illness is beneath me?*

Forces have been at work against me this week. I have been taking jobs from home. My cell will cut out in the middle of a business call, and I only realize this after talking to myself for 30 seconds. My email froze. The keyboard on my laptop stopped working. I had to complete 240 Google Analytics reports using the on-screen keyboard. Did your brain just explode? Geek Squad will probably block my number. One laptop adapter fried, the other is in a perpetual state of trying to find itself. *Who am I if the admin account on my computer can't even be found?* I look up at the universe for the millionth time this year, trying to solve the riddle. *What do you want me to do with this new me, now rendered work-less?* I yell at the ceiling. *You do understand we have to eat, right? Sure, it's lovely to have a vacation, but this is what I know.* Now there's a kink in the hose.

The ceiling stays quiet. So, I laugh, call the ceiling the b-word; I cry the tiniest bit when my family is out running errands. I make everyone sick to death of me. Me struggling is a prickly pear. I get it. But this prickly pear is lonely. This prickly pear is puzzled. *What is my next step already? Show me so I can conquer the world.*

Back to the visceral plan, which encompasses eating and breathing and ensuring those involuntary systems stay up and running. You can do this. When you have to keep going, do the best you can every day. Sometimes it's just breathing while practicing grace. Despite what anyone says, move forward in that best way even if you only travel an inch. Forgive yourself for not being as collected as you usually are.

Confronting one's mortality can have that effect. All sick people know that. Well people don't. Let's call them wellies. *It's OK. Wellies are not supposed to understand,* I remind myself. *They are merely supposed to try. It is all they will accomplish, and it is their role.* I'm not saying lower your expectations but adjust them.

Each day is new. Each night is a time of reflection. What was learned, done, planned? How did my body perform? Did I have one of my good days, or bad? Did I tell you illness is very selfish? Oh, yes indeedy, if you are the ailing one, take that news in. Each uncontrollable mess of a moment is a lesson in letting go. You might call me a reluctant Zen artist, sitting at the canvas attempting to paint peace, when I want to fall back on what's old and comforting, even if it is toxic. I want to paint trees in a pile of tinder, victims of a brutal storm. I want to paint blue, weary souls, breaking and healing hearts, misunderstanding, and strife. The usual nonsense of my past life. Not this happiness I am *supposed* to be feeling and for which *I am supposed to be grateful...* no matter how stupid-contagious it is.

But some days, the joy rushes in and suffocates me. I have felt the most purpose in my life this year. My calling is slowly taking shape, as if revealed through a veil.

No one can do your life work. No one can take your impor-tance away unless you let them. No one can force you to do, feel, be, anything. You are you, in your very personalized battle of life. Not one person is more interested in your success than you. Your caring should be enough because it is enough.

However you are fighting these emotional changes due to illness, a layoff, a divorce, a death, an accident, or tragedy, refusing to drown as tumultuous waves eclipse your life, you are doing it right. Because you are surviving. Even if you're wild, drenched, waving your arms, and screaming while beating at the torrents coming for you, if you are still sucking in air, you got it.

All we can do is move forward with the best of intentions and with our unique capabilities and limitations. I don't care what anyone else says, this is living in all its ugly glory, even if at times it resembles white-knuckle surviving. It's living with new limits.

Chapter 17

WHY YOU NEED TO QUESTION EVERY OPPORTUNITY IN BUSINESS

Business was clicking and whirring along. Leads were crawling out of the woodwork. I had tapped into a magical source capable of giving endlessly, and if you want to know the secret so that you, too, can experience the glorification of busyness, it's simple. Say "yes" to everything.

But, I should issue a caveat. There are times when saying "yes!" should be embraced. When someone needs your help and you are able to give of yourself without suffering detriment. When doing so allows for learning and the old adage of balancing risk versus reward tips toward the gift. When you are propositioned to take on a task you know you are capable of doing, or at the very least, you have the tenacity to figure out.

Then say "YES!"

Sometimes we say "yes" because we are fearful, because we have been conditioned to regard every chance as if it were an opportunity.

Chance and opportunity are two different things.

Mindlessly accepting what appear to be godsends from people in the form of sales, referrals, bartered deals, etc. isn't wise.

Consider this analogy: *If you are a loan officer and I send a prospect to you who is interested in buying a house, you still need to run their credit, don't you?*

It's exactly the same in business, which is why it is critical to perform your due diligence. Research that new contact. Take a look at their site, what they stand for. Learn how they respond to you (or don't). Assess what you agree with and what you would have a hard time working alongside. Be true to yourself when you answer the question of if you can work together.

Struggling against your heart is not sustainable.

Being on a different energy wavelength is enough of a discerning factor. No one knows you like you. No one has the intimate understanding of the processes you need to stay happy. Do you require more silence than noise? Do you need the positive collaboration of others working toward a goal? What are your specialties? Maybe you never want to work with a client in retail. Perfectly fine. You don't need validation to make your decision; you just need to operate from the standpoint of what works for you.

Then fearlessly live it.

We try so hard to emulate others who seem to have it all, but we know nothing of their lives. We have zero information on what their day looks like or how they really feel about the direction their business is going. We only know what is presented to us.

Make a promise to yourself to stop imitating others, to stop comparing yourself and your individual talents. Gauge yourself based on *the reason you are here*…the actions only you can deliver in your unique way.

Then, offer that service to a select few, those who pass your criteria and whose collaboration will likely lead to a positive and prosperous relationship. Refer anyone else who doesn't fit in with your vision and method.

The place to start? Get to know you. Write down what kind of work makes your soul sing. What types of personalities do you prefer to be around? What businesses set fire to your soul? What is your mission in working? Do you have a bigger purpose than running a business? If you're operating a nonprofit, you do. Has it been forgotten because of the fear of loss? Have you identified your service? At the end of the day, it all harkens back to the touchy-feely.

What you need may not be what someone else is looking for.

A referral, a project, a lead...these are all rudimentary starts, the vague shapes of potential. Flesh them out with cellular intention to learn what's right for you. Only when you can say "yes" will you realize the true gift of being unafraid to speak a loud and clear, guilt-free "no."

Chapter 18

HOW TO TURN ANXIETY INTO PRODUCTIVITY AND HAVE THE MOST EXPLOSIVE YEAR OF YOUR LIFE

I repeated my mantra…"You are not going to die. You are going to get busy."

Anxiety is a bugger. Let me start by acknowledging that. I could list the million little ways it tries to kill me, but I think those are more obvious than the gift I have only recently begun to see. Wedged deep inside anxiety (and as is the case with any challenge, IMO) was a tool. I just had to dig to get to it.

They say education is the cure to fear. I am a smart person. I am logical. I can cognitively understand the physiological thievery taking place in my body. I know that inching your way out of a panic attack requires longer breaths. This is all understandable until I am charged with taking those breaths as I struggle not to suffocate. Yes, anxiety feels like death, and for decades, I thought there was nothing good about it. It was an inconsiderate bully barging into my life, sometimes at the behest of nothing at all. But I had to live with it. I had to get to know it, and in doing so, I found that my anxiety can actually provide a channel to supercharged productivity.

I stumbled upon this quite naturally in the sweaty, quivering grasp of an anxiety attack. I wanted to come to terms with what I was worrying about so, I could get over it. But it's not that simple, is it? I asked myself a question—*What is really bothering you?*—to get started, and after I answered that question honestly, my creativity took off! Suddenly, I was writing articles, plotting business strategies, and I rose up through the layers holding me down. My shaking stopped, and my nausea eased, and when that happened, I took deeper breaths that allowed the whole physical process to reroute.

I learned I was not going to die (again).

With that reassurance, I continued to busy myself with more tasks to keep my mind occupied because I also knew I was vulnerable in that moment to relapse into anxiety.

I had to charge ahead!

I was up late/early after filling pages of ideas and musings. After confronting the mouse I had made into a bear, my fears blown up to eclipse any hope of recovery from terror, I had made some serious headway toward acknowledging my feelings about events that had transpired and removing blocks from my path. Recording what I was feeling and working through the origin of those emotions enabled me to detect my own empowerment again.

Harnessing your anxiety is like plugging in an alternate energy source, and it accomplishes two things at once: 1) You WILL work out what the mad, gnarled ball of pain is that you are holding, and 2) It removes the obstacles to your goals. When these two happenstances collide and collaborate, then you free your mind to release the creative musings that have been dammed up.

The next time I could feel the telltale signs of pre-anxiety, I knew I had better get my mind busy. I started writing again. I picked up my sketch pad. I revisited the spreadsheet I keep with the list of ongoing tasks I need to complete for my business.

- Update website

- Create social media posts

- Write blog posts

- Send pitch off to amazing media site

- Review portfolio of potential writers

- Network with editor (at long-coveted magazine)

- Seal deals

And on it goes…

Instead of waiting for the other psychological shoe to drop and cripple any activity, leisure or professional, I repeated my mantra: *You are not going to die. You are going to get busy*. Then I followed through.

There have been times when it was more challenging to re-emerge from anxiety. I will admit that, and during those moments, I try as hard as I can to make my body comply with physical commands. *You are going to grab your laptop and open that spreadsheet. You are going to write a blog post about the topic that struck you two days ago.* I give myself permission to pause the emotions coursing through me to work on distractions and progress. Because I will still physically feel that way whether I am lying in bed, sitting up and plunking away, or connecting with a new business friend.

Since I have started doing this, the severity of my anxiety attacks has significantly lessened. I can only tell you my story and how I think the hidden gem of anxiety is hyper-focus and the super power to crush achievements. I can't authorize you to listen to me or take my advice; I can only share that I have a greater understanding of what I am capable of when I step back and view the whole picture. My pent-up energy can be used to wrack my body with agony and dread, or that same energy can be applied to taking a few more steps toward my personal and professional goals.

Maybe you want to try it yourself? And if you want to talk about it, I would love to hear from you.

Chapter 19

WHY ASCRIBING INTENT IS NOT SERVING ANYONE

Your worst beliefs about yourself shut down your ability to hear the truth of what people believe about you.

One of the best changes I have ever made in my life is when I refused to stop ascribing intent.

This is a top reason I love Facebook sometimes. It is an endless river of inspiration for my writing, and it ignited the spark to extrapolate on this topic…as it has for many others.

It was in a group where I read the words: ascribing intent. More specifically, in a comment thread, one of the responses was: "You're ascribing intent."

It was a laser light show in my brain. Not kidding.

Everything lit up, and all the bells and whistles went haywire.

For decades…I had ascribed intent. *I had assumed based on people's behaviors what they would say to me.*

It provided the validation I needed to support scary decisions like cutting people out of my life permanently.

Or the time I assumed that my friend with the sick baby was ignoring me.

I have used it to intercept what I thought would be an agonizing answer to hear…*Am I fired? Don't you love me?*

Ascribing Intention…

Robs us of the gift of being brave, of learning we can handle more than we thought, of finding out we are NOT forgettable.

We are not bad people.

The worst beliefs you have about yourself FEED your ascribed intentions.

Ascribing intent denies the person you are interacting with the right to share their feelings.

It denies you the ability to rehab more fully from your ancient wounds and self-limiting beliefs.

It is easier to believe the worst about ourselves than it is to hear the truth of how people view us.

We work so hard on beating ourselves up sometimes that we *believe* the terrible things our inner voice shouts at us.

They have found out I suck, and now they are severing ties.

They have found out I have emotions and am a master crazymaker.

They have found out that I make mistakes, and now they don't think I am good enough.

They have found out that I am a handful of drama and that outweighs any talents I think I have.

They have found out I have no special qualities…

That I worry.

That I am not as confident as I seem.

That I get tired, discouraged, beaten.

AND NOW

They want out.

Beating someone to the punch is the personification of ascribing intent.

Don't speak any further. I don't have the stomach to hear your painful truths about how awful I am. Even if it is couched in the nicest and thickest disclaimers.

Also…vice versa. Just as we assume how people feel about us, so too do people assume how we feel about them.

How many people have made assumptions about you? About what terrifies you? What moves you? The reason for your decision?

As I sat in our sunny backyard on a day when the stifling, humid air refused to move an inch, I knew I needed to cut the last tie with the person I was talking to on the phone… but I was so terrified to hear that I was going to be abandoned again, I couldn't allow myself to hear what the person was saying. It was my habit to break the connection before the other party could get to it because it was easier to be the one calling it quits than the one receiving the heave ho. They were talking, and I could listen to their words, but I couldn't allow them to be spoken. I knew what was coming. My volume rose as I sobbed over their conversation: "Don't say it. Don't say it. Don't say it." *If I just keep talking over them, I will never hear the ripping, the rending of one soul from another. I will never learn that my worst fear is true…I am forgettable forever.*

In that instance, I was right…it was horrendous. Sometimes it is. But that is still no excuse not to face fear and listen. It is no excuse to create noise and disruption because panic surges through you.

Be calm. Hear what is being said to you. Emotions will crash on your sensory shoreline. Stand there and take it. Remember, you don't have to say anything…yet or ever. But listen. This is your only job: to challenge yourself to hear what probably isn't as bad as what you have obsessed over and imagined.

And when you catch yourself on the other end, when you are in the company of a panicked individual who just wants the confrontation to be over, understand that fear is driving the compulsion to shut you down.

The other day, I tried to quit on a client via text message. The crazy thing is, at the time, I thought I was handling the issue in an acceptable manner. I really did.

I had sat with the situation and not responded immediately. (In retrospect, I stewed.) I had thought that I was expected to be perfect at all times and that any imperfection meant I had no value.

I literally thought that I was not allowed to be human.

I had ordered myself to perform without any of the mess of being a person, of learning, of stretching and growing.

Nope, I told myself, *even though you tell other people to love themselves through their mistakes, you are not allowed to make them.*

Laymen's terms: you are to live a double standard.

No wonder I was such a wreck.

"Listen," I told my client and friend, "I freak out. I am afraid people will walk away, and I just want you to know that because when it happens…well, can you help reel me back in?"

In the olden days of office yore, you would *never* allow any "weakness" to show. Maybe that is why when I needed to feel heard, I would scream it out and then be shown the door.

Now, we can confess our humanness and realistically expect to be embraced *because of our "flaws" and honesty.*

No more ascribing intention and usurping the right of another person to express themselves. You or me, OK?

When we stop, when we refuse to partake of the visceral response of fear, then we also learn the beautiful softness of hearing true intention.

It is freeing to learn most people are *not* intentionally trying to hurt you.

That they may be ascribing intention themselves.

That ascribing intention mucks up how communication works.

And it is easier to get over a supposed wrong when you learn and accept that most hurts are not deliberate. That people make mistakes and, just like you and me, should be allowed the opportunity to screw up without damage to their confidence.

We all make mistakes. We all live with that occasional (or more frequent) scolding voice in our heads, and it takes pure adrenaline to shut out what we believe will be the confirmation of our worst selves.

Are you hanging in limbo just waiting to hear how awful you are? That other people will learn this about you and then the ruse will be up? You will be outed?

When we stop ascribing intention, we learn this is not the case. That we are not so bad after all. I promise.

We learn that there is NO ONE out there hell-bent on hating us or destroying us by a thousand nicks…usually.

If you discover this is not the case, obviously address that toxicity and build a moat that the toxic person cannot cross.

But in Everydayland, texts, emails, tones are misread constantly.

It is time to hear the truth.

It is courageous to apply the relevant pieces we learn about ourselves toward our own betterment.

When we do, we erase stigmas, assumptions, divisions, and fear.

Simply by refusing to ascribe intention.

We deepen connections and collaboration. We honor that trust is hard-earned and serious. We believe there are more good people than bad.

We develop brighter observations about the world, about ourselves and our abilities.

We *change* our assumptions and begin to believe what we never thought we could: We *are* good enough. Worth the time. Engaging. Valuable. An asset to every area of our life.

It is the best surprise you can't imagine.

We swap out our destructive thought patterns as we help others do the same.

One of my authors reminded me that we have two ears and one mouth.

I think he's onto something.

Chapter 20

THE INSIDIOUS DANGER OF THE SCARCITY MIND-SET

It's time to wield the sword of conscious compassion in the battle against the scarcity mind-set…in business, in family, in LIFE. It's time to recapture what is rightfully ours, the belief that we are valuable people.

It creeps on you…the scarcity mind-set. Your words form from its lush, black depths. It coils into your brain and shoots out of your mouth, becomes your thoughts, veers you in another direction before you even see it coming. It's a chameleon hunkering in the shadows, and when doubt forms in your fathomless recesses, you hear it…in the tones of your voice. It takes over your accountability, makes hope in yourself fade to a tattered whisper.

I hear people gripped in its talons. "Why doesn't he like me?" *Because you fear your value is scarce.* "Why won't the client sign?" *Because some leading part of your communication is drowning in scarcity, is coaxing the outcome to failure…this happens when you think you are not worth much.*

Definitely not a catch.

When we think of, or when we read about, the scarcity mind-set, a majority of people likely reference their business experiences. They may liken the theory to the exact opposite of the abundance mind-set, and while I am a little "woo-woo," yeah...the abundance mind-set is real.

You have heard that your thoughts inform your decisions, and therefore...they also create your life.

It's true.

You cannot and will not find the best version of yourself if your opinion of yourself is damaging or hopeless or if you are fearful.

You will be held back because your belief will not allow you to advance. No matter how many times you wish and wish and wish to make progress on that rutted road.

The scarcity mind-set overlaps into the conditions of our lives. When you look at people who are happy in the various core areas of life—family, career, spirituality, for starters—a theme emerges. Their faith in themselves is spread across the intersections of these elements. It is virtually impossible to believe in your potential in one segment of your life yet execute with dubious undertones in another. Not with full and robust confidence anyway.

Because the scarcity mind-set is self-sabotaging, it is also circular. It keeps you trapped unless you do the hard work to break free of the loop.

Begin with changing your thoughts…one small alteration. Apply it. Try this out (as read from a meme): Stop complaining for 24 hours. You will not hear your voice. You will exercise control over your words, and as you do, the belief that you are the one at the wheel will embolden you until you DO realize you are the captain.

Refusing to complain aloud has a wondrous effect on our insides, too. Call it an effect of the truncated negative energy that you have effectively shut down, but when you refuse to wail aloud, it swaps the record in your mind. This statement I overheard hits me: "Maybe you are healed from hearing what other people said to you, whatever hurt you… but you still had to hear it." It continues to ring out. The same holds true for your own voice…when you listen to it. And when you stop it.

This refusal to embrace the darker side of circumstance reboots your inner world, too.

How do I know?

I spent many years blaming a shitty childhood for the fact that I couldn't catch a break in my career, in love, in LIFE. I spent many years trying to be what I thought others wanted me to be…and *of course*, I failed. Because I was not aiming for goals of my own making. So, I simply stopped. It works.

A ray of light infiltrated my head and disintegrated my shadows. I stopped complaining. I said things like, "I'm sorry," "I'm responsible," "I hurt you," instead. When I took ownership, it transformed every detail I had ever fretted over.

When you take ownership of your words and actions, you also take ownership of a deeper meaning within you…of who you are. You reinforce your goodness, your strengths, your right to be human and to express frailty without condemnation. And so…when events take a dip, you don't panic. Instead you issue a little self-love, slather on a dollop of forgiveness, squirt out a dab of wisdom, applying it liberally…and life goes on.

My life is vastly different because I opened myself to living without scarcity. There is nothing of scant supply in my existence and guess what? There is nothing lacking in yours either.

You are perfect as a stumbling, triumphant, vulnerable, trying, reaching human. And so is everybody freakin' else.

When you embark on a project, when you plan a date, when you interact with your family, do so knowing your worth; do so believing people love you because you deserve it. And be harsh in defending your right to live this way. Those who do not love you in the way you need do not get to go any further with you. Boundaries, always a good thing. Announce your edict to sever ties, absent of emotion and filled with peace…be it in business or pleasure.

So, you…embrace life in all its charming ugliness and love yourself anyway. Believe you are a force who is resilient enough to take a few tough hits. You are impenetrable. You will stand the test of time. You can survive entombed in a landfill for twenty-thousand years.

And no matter what, never cede your ability to enjoy your life to self-doubt based in history, childhood, divorce, alienation, abandonment, enablement, or any other "ment" or experience.

The abundance mind-set will open doors, through sheer belief. The sheer belief becomes the fuel to obtain what you desire, and that is what leads to the ultimate parade of entrances just waiting for you to enter. These doors of varied opportunity are yours, but you won't find them if you live eclipsed within the scarcity mind-set.

Conversely, adopting abundance as your go-to approach ensures your deepest confidence soars in synergy with your outward actions, and so, you win more. More love. More proliferation of whatever you want: increased revenue, professional opportunities, the influence to sway events and opinions. Whatever grows from confidence becomes inevitable reality.

Chapter 21

INTRODUCING SICK BIZ

When I lost my job, I remember feeling incredibly helpless. It was a time when no amount of out-working, out-talking, out-riding, or out-anything else was going to help me. I had dreamed of being an entrepreneur for decades. I had seen my father take innumerable stabs at entrepreneurship and fail. This left an awful taste in my mouth, and I recoiled as I ascertained, *You shouldn't work for yourself. It's not a viable option, and there is no guarantee that you will get paid, that you will be able to feed your children, that you can make your house payment, your car payment, or all your bills. The only guarantee appears to be that struggle, pain, frustration, and self-doubt will plague you.*

I had no choice because untenable physical challenges like vertigo, burning, tingling, numbness, dead limbs, murderous eyeball pain, and excruciating fatigue were my new constant companions. So, in January 2015, I turned what had been a part-time venture marketing business into a full-time personification of prayer. I balanced my new endeavor with heavy unemployment benefits that lasted about nine months before they dried up. By that time, I had landed a national hotel chain as a client and was working on multiple monthly projects. I remained at every person's digital doorstep, begging, bartering, cajoling, and groveling for any jobs that were severely under my pay scale. I didn't care because in my estimation I was going to do the work. Monday was going to come, and our living would not be interrupted. Because I'd destroyed my children's families through multiple divorces, this one pledge my tattered mind understands: My children will not experience the loss of leaving their school with all their friends. I would do everything in my power to try and ensure we didn't need to move. We've only moved twice in their lifetimes. That fact makes me proud.

I dug into survivor mode to get this business off the ground and worked as hard as I possibly could, but I could only work part-time. I was still enduring the sensory disruptions in my body from having a damaged thoracic spinal cord and a lesion that, although very small, is located on top of bundles of nerves affecting both my upper and lower motor control. I still have symptoms neurologists cannot correlate to any specific lesion in my body. I guess it will just be that way.

When I was not working part-time, I had to nap and give my body a chance to heal by regenerating cells and calming inflammation. I went from not being able to clean the kitchen for five months to tackling chores in chunks. It seemed I was coming back from the brink of not knowing whether I would live or die. My first and only active flare of my disease, that had torn the myelin away on my spinal cord, was starting to affect me with less symptomatic intensity. I was astounded to hear the news I was healing and stabilizing.

I was entering into a phase of recovery and likely creating new scarring that would live on my spinal cord forever, meaning my life could get a little bit more predictable. I required less sleep than I had and could control my symptoms to some degree—feeling crappy only about 70% to 80% of the time versus feeling horrendous and unable to function, walk, focus, remember, or even sit upright 99% of the time. A lot of this pain management came through dietary changes, increased sleep, safeguarding myself from colds and flu, decreasing stress, and trying to maintain a body temperature that wouldn't leave me freezing or scorching hot.

Still, I had to accept my new condition and rewrite the rules for success. And I continue to rewrite them because the entrepreneur space puts a heavy emphasis on competing. But you can't compete at the same level as someone who is "healthy." You have to redesign the game, redesign the relays, the handoffs, and the structure of your day, and boil it down to productivity goals in hours. You have to maximize your efficiency, and you have to enlist time hacks that will help you complete projects more quickly without losing quality.

I continued to work in this capacity for about a year and a half, and I networked every single day. I have lost track of the number of emails I've sent. When you are down and can't find work, when your life changes and you don't have any money, make a list. Write down 250 people you can email even if you haven't talked to them in 12 years, as I have previously mentioned. Explain where you are at in your life, what has changed, what you are trying to accomplish, and acknowledge that you know it is completely weird you're reaching out to them after so much time. Tell them you need their help and you hope they will be open to working with you. Don't send a template letter. Remember, you have all the time in the world right now. Jobs aren't coming in, and people aren't pounding on your inbox trying to work with you. One connection can change your life and your present state. When you start working for someone and they are delighted with what you can bring and the value that you can give them, you will increase the value in your life and your offerings.

I want to pause here and make sure you understand our goal is value first. When you approach people with the intention to deliver value and talk about how excited you are to be working with them, that it is an honor, and when you backup your words with action, people will adore working with you. When you are working with a company you have long coveted, always be grateful, always be value-oriented no matter what. Remember, this is their project, their initiative; this is their brain child that you are privileged to collaborate on.

One day, I wrote a press release for a skanky PR company that wanted me to feature a very intriguing gentleman and the person who wrote the foreword of this book, Ryan Stewman. I saw that Ryan had endured the same type of existence I had and immediately felt a connection to him and an unspoken bond. We'd both survived repeated pain derived from suffering, screwing up, failing, trying again, losing everything, coming back, and through it all, looking in the mirror and assigning the responsibility to ourselves. I read Ryan's book *Hardcore Closer* in less than one night and discovered he had written more books. I reached out to him after having written his press release and speaking to his wife, and she loved it, and then he loved it, and so I felt that gave me the opening to nudge the door a crack further. I proposed that I should be his editor and that not only should I edit *Hardcore Closer*, but I would edit all his books. Then, we began working together. Our relationship wasn't without challenges, and at one point we almost parted ways. But then I realized I needed to get as vulnerable as I had gotten with my husband.

I was finally receiving acceptance as a person even though I was offering very little value in terms of money, housework, emotional support, etc. It was shocking to discover: I needed to do even *more* emotional work. In my personal life, I had achieved a relationship that was thriving, honest, and open, that brought me such happiness and provided security, but I had yet to implement this practice into my professional life.

All my life, I have been afraid of confrontation. So much so that even those moments the majority of people might deem to be a mild altercation or difference of opinion accelerate my heartbeat. Sometimes I would ghost people and leave without saying a word. In the past, when I had been fired, I had not spoken up or made a peep, but merely picked up my box of office belongings to step alongside security. I drifted before anyone even knew I had left.

I knew this was not the way to grow. I needed to enter into an additional level of healing that I desired to have in my life. I wanted to get better. I wanted to have open conversations with people and even delve into subjects that were uncomfortable. I wanted to talk as mature adults.

Ryan and I both had some growing to do in the early stages because we pretty much blew up at each other. But then we tried it again, and I credit him and our ability to keep trying to the progress I have made in my business. Instead of questioning him and his motives, I shut my mouth, did what I was told, and then applied what he was telling me to do for his business to my own business.

I began to grow a following.

I never stopped networking, and since I was editing all of his blogs, I was privy to his mastermind epiphanies. I was privy to his growth and the lessons he was learning. This was especially true when I was editing his books. Instead of believing I needed to have control in my business relationships, I began to see that I had been a poor manager in my past work. Because the control and the status had mattered too much. I was not focused on the person. I was not focused on leading in a positive manner to allow for collaborative growth, confidence, and further innovation. I was centered on the high it gave me to be the boss because, for the first time in my life, people paid attention to me.

So, I did what he told me to do. I assigned myself a weekly column to keep myself accountable in my writing goals and to gift myself a piece of media I could share. I asked for connections and in exchange offered worth. I reached out to people I didn't know and requested to be their friend, and then I didn't ask anything of them but to hang out. I commented on their posts and engaged in a genuine relationship with them even though I had previously been advised to strike up relationships with people in powerful positions and leverage those relationships to serve me. But that felt wrong and deceitful. It wasn't authentic to who I am, which is a person who brings value first.

From my contact with Ryan, stepping out on that branch and asking for his business, I pushed myself to heal from prior trust issues as I had done in my personal relationships.

But this time, my business relationships underwent rehab. When I saw it was possible to recuperate in my personal life, I wanted the same dynamic in my business interactions.

Ryan began to send me referrals for editing books. I had not thought of offering this service for my business, and in fact, my business was a bit muddy to outsiders. My services were not niche; they were not well-defined. They covered too many bases and not enough specialties, and I had a very hard time letting go of some of the services that filled me with bliss. For instance, I thought I could offer graphic design services. And for a while, I did. But this wasn't my aptitude, and I wasn't maximizing my time or profit by engaging in a task that wasn't my strength, and so now I outsource that to my delightful, wonderful graphic designer and close friend, Christine Dubay. I redeveloped my company. I eradicated anything that did not have to do with copywriting, copy editing, or book editing, and recently I've added the service of coaching writers in developing their books.

Positioning myself as an expert instead of as a business, I worked with people who wanted to engage with me on projects, despite the fact I believed I gave scarce value. Instead, I did the best I could over and over and over and over and over again as I worked in the same concentrations. By doing this, I reinforced the message I was an expert in select fields only. And I can write, draw, or indulge in any creative activity anytime I want. My ability to do so is not limited because I don't provide graphic design services.

I'm reassigning these services because they don't have a place in my business. As I continued working in my marketing company, bringing on clients, editing books, and copywriting for large corporations and entrepreneurs, I especially helped to develop and monetize blogs.

As I grew, I thought of how far I had come from the shriveled heap in the bed who wondered if she was months away from dying.

By that time, I recognized and accepted I couldn't return to a traditional work environment. But I also didn't want to. To a large degree, I had beat the specter looming over my head, arising from failed, nightmarish entrepreneurships. I didn't know if I wanted to return to work for a corporation even though I knew I couldn't. Had I been given a choice I would have continued to work for myself and to build my own empire and my own miracles every day.

Miracles don't have to be so monumental or biblical. But it is a miracle when you work for yourself daily and create elements and projects of your own doing or of a group's doing.

As I reflect on the journey I have been on and what led me to my success, I know success is never stagnant. Success is not a destination and then a ceasing-to-be. When I lost my job, I didn't have the support or the professional tools to know where to begin making a living wage, much less a glamorous wage, or to even compete with other healthy entrepreneurs. These people had at their advantage the ability to operate on less sleep, the ability to push themselves harder without physical disintegration. But I was doing it regardless of my slim odds. I was accomplishing milestones.

With my bearings underneath me, I couldn't wait to breathe life into an idea I'd had to help other entrepreneurs like me. It was my turn to give back. I wanted people to know that if you had the tools and the training needed to strengthen your business, life, money, and mental health, you could make more than a living wage. You could make a reputation for yourself that would keep paying off. The nonprofit Sick Biz is that resource for you.

Sick Biz has been operational since approximately July 2017, and in that time, we have had a website built for us through the generosity of my friend Robert Wiesman and his team. Our arrangement started as bartering, but Robert simply refused to ever send work back my way, and now he is the producer of the *Sick Biz Buzz* podcast, my voice coach, and a very dear friend. I could not have done any of this without Robert. We have since assembled a board of directors, and there's more work to be done to give people the chance to help, heal, encourage, and empower themselves through their health and business challenges.

Through my research, I have learned that the CDC estimated in 2014 that half of Americans have a chronic illness.[3] Having a chronic illness and managing the daily physical challenges that are always fluctuating is very difficult, especially in terms of keeping up your end of the bargain that you will report to work at the same time and that you will work 8, 9, or 10 hours a day. When you work for someone else, there is zero flexibility in changing up times, so you can rest, and when you can't adapt to how you need to work, you can't find comfort. You can't prolong stamina. So, it would appear there's a huge number of chronically ill and disabled people, as well as people undergoing temporary treatments for cancer and other diseases that leave them unable to work outside their home. We needed a nonprofit to assist these people in reaching their business goals and helping them continue to work.

As of this publication, we have 20 + guest bloggers on SickBiz.com. Our podcast, *Sick Biz Buzz*, airs weekly with the tagline, "It's the sickest podcast empowering chronically ill and disabled entrepreneurs." People listen. They find a place of acceptance. Our Facebook group has nearly

3. Markus MacGill, "Half of All American Adults Have a Chronic Disease—CDC," *Medical News Today*, July 2, 2014, https://www.medicalnewstoday.com/articles/279084.php.

1,000 people, and members are grateful to be a part of it because they feel they have found support in others who understand their situations. These are people just like them.

I hope this book will urge you to unearth your own astounding abilities to create your own everyday miracles. I want you to live and work in a business that is highly profitable and rewarding.

Please feel free to reach out to me and engage with our Sick Biz community to receive the help that you need, clarify the direction you want to go, and get in contact with experts in our field who can assist you in reaching your most exciting goals.

As you turn the final page, remember that you matter. Your past does not dictate your future.

Remember, as my friend, who feels more like a brother, said today: "Hil-Dawg, before you can move on to the next phase of your journey, before you can board the next airplane, if you haven't unpacked from your prior trip you can't move ahead." (Ironically, he shared this brain nugget with me as he waited for his connecting plane in an airport.) He went on: "I can't take what I brought with me on my earlier trip on this trip. Instead, I have to unpack everything from my past and from my bag. I have to do that to move forward. These are the actions that you need to take to move forward in your life, too. Unpack your history. Lay it all out on the bed and see your journey for what it was, what it is, and what you thought it was. Figure out what you learned and what you should take responsibility for. Then put it all away somewhere after you acknowledge what you have learned and the feelings that have arisen from it. After you have worked through those feelings, you will get to a place of closure. Only then can you stow those items away in a place where you know where they are, but you don't need to see them every day. You need new items in your bag now for a different trip that calls for different expectations and different goals to be met. These new items will be useful in meeting different people. And you will add new stories to your life." He paused, and I could almost picture his eyes narrowing in, concentrating, as he left me with his last thought: "But you cannot take any further or more enthralling trips until you unpack your last bag." And then he sent me off on my way to finish this book for you.

If you are tired, bone-weary, exhausted from carrying around pain, revisit the lessons, the actionable steps, as many times as you need so that you can move past such paralyzing agony, doubt, and lack of self-care. Let this book be your guide and apply healing not only to your business but to your experiences. You don't have to be indebted to the mistakes you made before you knew better. Take responsibility for them but stop pummeling yourself because you only had the tools you had developed at that time in your toolbox. You didn't even know you needed a different tool to advance. You don't get to chastise yourself for being unaware that you needed a hacksaw instead of a table saw. That's not fair to you. I can look back on certain situations that ended with separation and know now that the people involved (including myself) did not have the tools to work together. We were too busy trying to care for ourselves. To survive. And only this past year have I begun to understand my "abandonment." I don't see people leaving as a deliberate action to hurt me; I see it as the inability to problem-solve based on tragic circumstances. Think of hummingbirds in a small room. They are knocking into each other and falling down. They can't help each other because all they know is baseline stimulation— it's how they are wired and is similar to how people can be stress-programed—now they have spiked their anxiety by being placed in the box. All they are thinking (and that is a strong word, as they might not have the capability of deliberating) about is getting out of that box intact. They can't attend to the other birds. And no other birds will assist them. Not a very useful situation, is it? But while the feathers fly and one bird after another gets out, the separation between all happens. It is then you realize the focus was only on getting out alive. The nurturing of any other relationship was not possible; it could not have been given the time for nourishment and development, and so it remains shallow with an undercurrent of hurt and hypersensitivity. The memory that remains is one of panic and subsequent isolation. It is not of togetherness or unity.

Thank you for reading about my journey. Thank you for pausing in your day to take care of yourself and to think about what you need in your life. I hope my stories inspired you and ignited in you a long-lived persistence and drive. I hope they underscored the desire in you to do what you feel you need to do. For help, please visit SickBiz.com, send an email to SickBizCo@gmail.com, or text Sick Biz to 36260 to install our app on your phone.

People are waiting to help you move into the next phase of your life. This is exactly why Sick Biz was founded. For you.

ACKNOWLEDGMENTS

The theory is that an author should not gush in their acknowledgments, but I am one to break the rules. So, here we go.

First, to my husband, who listens for ridiculously long periods to every thought stampeding through my head. Who picks me up when I get rattled and somehow finds a way to extract the belief that I can do it from a kernel of my withered self. You know my language, my heart, my spirit, and every vulnerability. I am so honored that you are my person and I am yours. I love you endlessly.

To my kiddos, Josh, Colton, and Lauren. You endured so much and taught me it was so easy to parent. I just needed to love you no matter what. I have, and I do. Your unconditional love allowed me to believe I was worth something. I am so blessed to love you and be your mom.

Shawn Doyle, you read one of my Facebook posts and then connected me with Sound Wisdom. I would not be typing on this page if it weren't for you. You were willing to share your own success and joy with me. I am grateful. Rachael, I am so thankful for your warm friendship and acceptance, which I felt the instant I met you.

David Wildasin, you have made this project incredible in many ways. I love that I can talk to you like a human and not a media mouthpiece, you are always brimming with encouragement and brainstorms. Thank you for believing in my message.

Nathan Martin, when I met you in Long Beach, you helped to reinflate the belief that I was not whistling in the wind. Thank you for including me in your vision.

The Sound Wisdom team for your patience as I silently freaked out and tried to deliver. Thank you for being steadfast.

Ryan Stewman, my thanks are never enough. My words are inadequate. You have changed my entire existence. I love you, my friend and brother of choice.

Robert Wiesman, I love your face off! You have hopped into this business with me and done everything in your power to blow up brand awareness, encourage me every step of the way, and laugh in hysterics with me as much as possible. Sick Biz is still alive because of you. I can't thank you enough!

Mat Bodhi Bryan, your ability to heal and teach others this same heart regeneration resulted in an astounding conversation, article, and book chapter. You poured fuel onto the fire of my calling. I see you doing what you're doing, and I think, *me too.*

The Good Men Project, you were my first stage and gave rise to the belief that I could write. I am indelibly connected to you and grateful.

Influencive, your site is a renaissance-reinvention, devoted to providing the most thought-provoking and meaningful content. Thank you for your unflagging faith and the space you offer to all your writers.

The Mighty, for recognizing the need to tell true stories of people living with chronic illness. So many have found a place where they can just be themselves because of you.

To the readers and the people suffering silently and out loud, I believe in you. You deserve every bit of good. Find your voice and share your story to leave a legacy of helping others. Every day, begin your mental calisthenics by telling yourself you should have blessings and love showered upon you. Say it often, and you will believe it. Thank you for riding shotgun on this trip.

ABOUT THE AUTHOR

Freelance Minnesota writer, author, and die-hard word nerd, Hilary Jastram reads grammatical reference books in her spare time. She is the author of *Killing Karl*, a story about a career killer masquerading as an everyday man, and his wife trying desperately to love him. She also operates J. Hill Marketing & Creative Services, specializing in copywriting and editing/coaching resources for up-and-coming writers and Fortune 500 brands. She cannot stop writing. For there is no control over love. And that is what writing is…love. Like any other passion.

In 2017, Hilary founded Sick Biz, a nonprofit dedicated to providing support, resources, hope, and hacks to chronically ill and disabled entrepreneurs. The *Sick Biz Buzz*, podcast soon followed, and even more incredible resources are in development.

Hilary lives in Champlin, Minnesota, with her husband and daughter, and she is also the mother to two grown sons. Although she lives with the inconsiderate disease, transverse myelitis, her emotional state has never been more robust. Connect with Hilary on her website SickBiz.com, and text Sick Biz to 36260 to download the Sick Biz app on your phone.